What this Book is all about

Cryptography is everywhere in our digital life

One of the best skills that you can gain if you're a developer, or working in the cybersecurity, information technology industry, or even a curious person, is cryptography

Securing our information is used all over, it is essential to your work, and it is far more fun than it seems

You will learn of secret keys and understand how encryption works, and the concepts behind it

"**Book Of Secrets**", will walk you through the most important cryptographic concepts from the classic era up until now. we will look at different use cases and learn how encryption and cryptanalysis work.

This book is a fascinating journey to one of the most secret and unknown skill

Every chapter includes hands-on practices

It is written for beginners and intermediate users

Table Of Contents

What this Book is all about	1
Table Of Contents	4
An Exercise	7
Cryptography Essentials	12
Basic Terminology	18
Substitution	26
Transposition	27
Caesar cipher	29
Brute Force	39
Brute Force Table	43
Bits, Permutations, and reversible Map	45
CryptAnalysis	51
Playfair Cipher	60
Vigenere cipher	68
Breaking Vigenere Cipher	72
Autokey Cipher	72
Transposition Ciphers	76
Jefferson cipher wheel	81
One-Time Pad	87
True Random	90

Moving to Binary	91
Random Numbers	96
Entropy	97
True And Pseudo	102
True Random	103
Pseudo-Random	103
Hybrid Random Numbers	104
Your Own Algorithm	105
Symmetric Encryption	110
Stream Cipher	112
Encrypting Text	113
Block cipher	115
Modern Cipher - Algorithm operation	120
Asymmetric Encryption	124
Generate Public and Private Key	129
Final Words	133

An **Exercise**

let's start with a question

You Enter your office and you need to enter a **4**-character password the keypad has **10** digits

"How many **password possibilities** are there? "

Using basic math, The answer is **10 to the power of 4 (you multiply 10 by itself 4 times)**

$$10^4$$

This question actually leads to some basic crypto terminology

- The **secret key** complexity is **10** digits from **0-9**
- The **key length** is **4** characters
- The **keyspace**, the number of possibilities is **10,000** combinations

You will read and learn of these terms all over this book.

When we deal with cryptography, the art of hiding things, anyone knows what is the cipher algorithm that generated the cipher message. But the attacker/hacker tries to find out what is the **secret key**

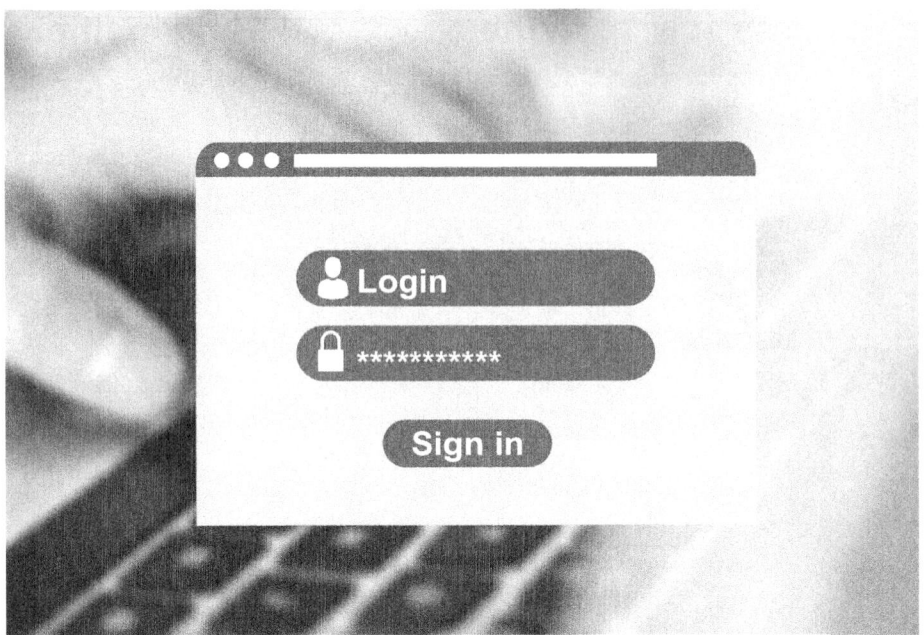

When it comes to **passwords as used on our computers**, the basic and minimum policy is to enter **8** characters.

Since the English alphabet has **26 characters**, that leads to a complexity of **52** characters (**26** upper-case and **26** lower-case)

Using the same technique as before leads to:

- Key complexity of 52 characters
- A key length of 8 characters
- Key space of 53,459,728,531,456

$$52^8$$

Cryptography Essentials

When we speak of cryptography, there is the **classic cryptography** with ciphers such as Caesar Cipher, Vigenere cipher, and the Playfair cipher

On the other side, we have **modern cryptography** which involves symmetric ciphers, asymmetric ciphers, hash functions so on.

We will look at each and we will understand the fundamentals behind each.

Cryptology

```
Cryptography          Cryptanalysis
     ↓                       ↓
Classic  Modern         Classic  Modern
   ↓       ↓
Transposition Substitution  Symmetric Asymmetric
```

When do we use cryptography?

We actually use it just about anywhere. We use it when we send messages, When we speak over IP, When we connect to a secure web server over HTTPS. We use it in our Wi-Fi to secure our Wi-Fi traffic.

Digital life and cryptography are combined together for the last 40 years, and of the most dominant use cases for using cryptography within the last 30 years is definitely our SmartPhones.

When we use voice calls, our data is **encrypted**

When we store data in our smartphones, it is **encrypted**.

When we browse web sites, the connection nowadays is usually **encrypted**

Why do we encrypt everything?

For two main reasons:
- The first one is confidentiality. We don't want anyone to take a look at our data and understand what is going on

- The second reason is authentication, We use encryption algorithms to produce digital signatures and certificates to make sure that the other side that we communicate with is indeed the one that we think

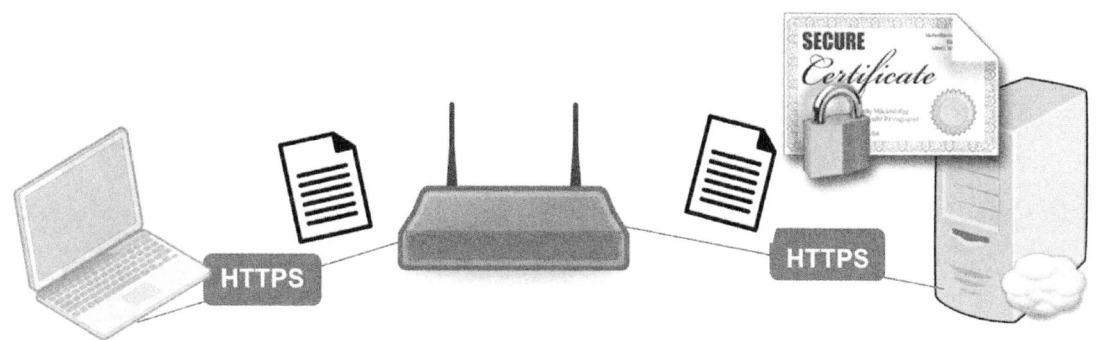

When do we encrypt?

We encrypt in 2 main scenarios, which we will look at in more detail as we go on and discuss block and stream ciphers

- When we store data (as in backups)
- When the data is in transit (travels through our networks as in messaging apps or browsing to a secure website)

Basic Terminology

Here are some of the basic terms that will be discussed throughout this book :

Plain Text - that is the original, text the original message.

Ciphertext - that is the encrypted message.

Encryption - is the process or function that turns the plaintext into ciphertext.

Decryption - on the other side is the reverse it restores the claim from the ciphertext.

Key is the information that is used within the encryption algorithm that is the cipher known only to the sender and to the receiver.

Cipher - is the algorithm that is the encryption algorithm and we will look at different encryption algorithms along with this book.

Cryptography is the study of algorithms that are used for encryption.

Encryption Process

Let's look at **Encryption and Decryption**

Encryption is actually a function that takes two inputs:
- A plaintext
- And the secret key

The process **(cipher algorithm) that takes the 2 inputs and manipulates them** can be quite complicated but it is usually common knowledge, the real challenge is the secret Key

The result is the **ciphertext,** The unrecognized text that is being sent to the other side

The recipient needs to know 2 things in order to decrypt the message :
- The encryption algorithm
- The key that was used to encrypt the plaintext

And the output is again, the **plain text.**

That is the process. So let's look at an example

Can you guess What are the ciphered words? What is the Plain Text That hides behind the ciphertext?

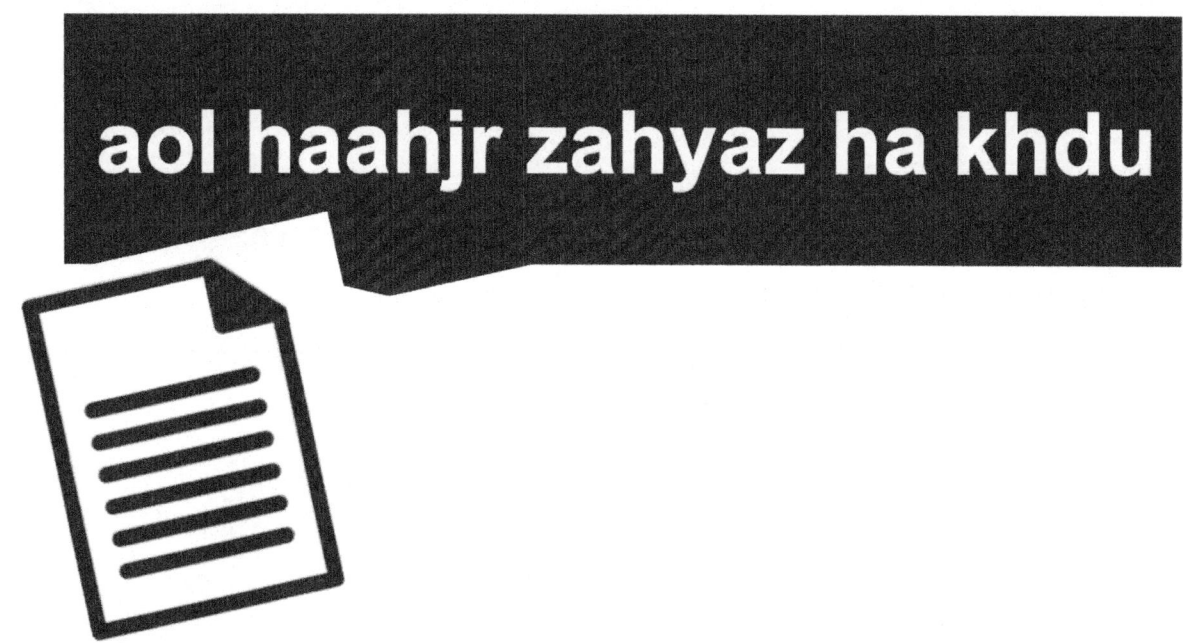

If you are not familiar with the secret key and the encryption algorithm, this would be quite difficult

The plaintext is actually the words **"the attack starts at dawn"**

The cipher algorithm that I'm using is **Caesar cipher known also as a shift cipher, or a substitute cipher, one of the oldest ciphers known. We will look at it very soon**

And the secret key is **Number 7**

Encryption Challenges

There are some encryption challenges that we have to face:

The first one is how do we generate secret keys

And the second one, which is much harder, is how do we deliver them between both sides

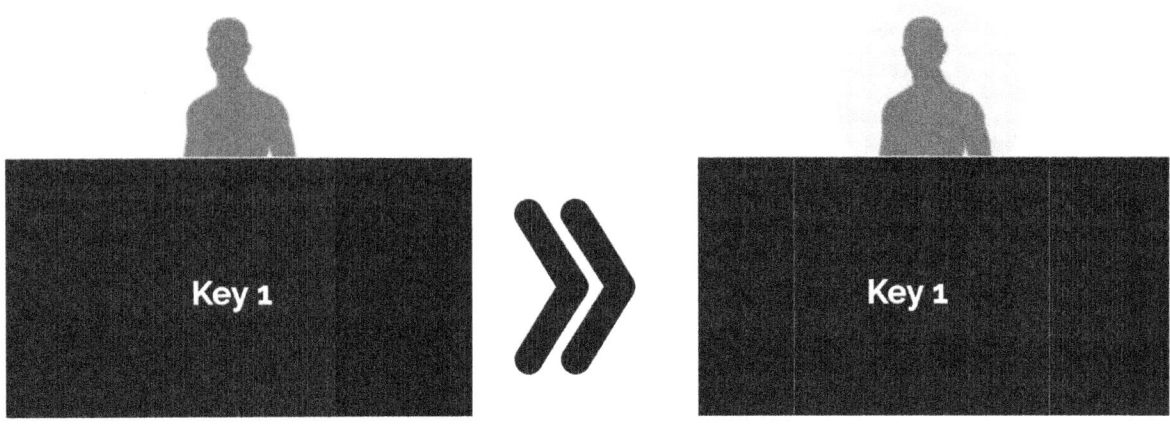

We will look at the different challenges later on.

Encryption algorithms use many techniques. the two most used are **Substitution** and **Transposition**.

Substitution

In **substitution**, we change **(Shift)** one element with another. Caesar Cipher uses substitution. We change an alphabet letter or group of letters with another letter according to a fixed method.

For example, if the method substitutes the letters **2 places**

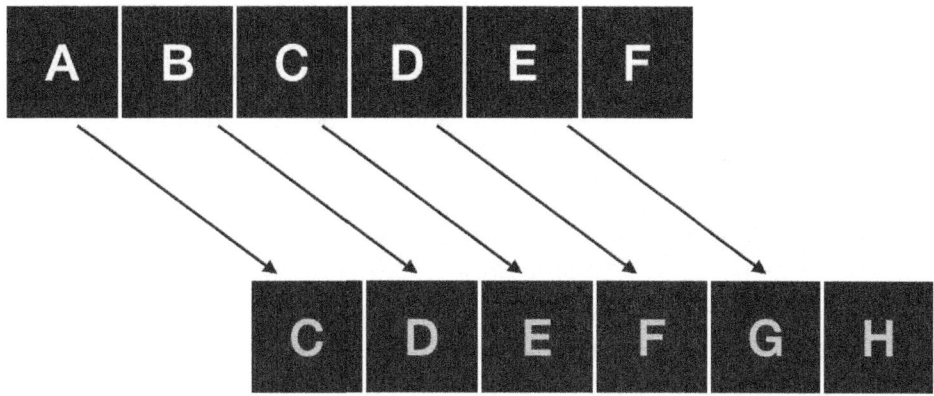

A becomes **C**, **B** becomes **D**, and so on. You can play with the shift number

There are several types of **substitution** techniques and ciphers that use this technique :

Simple Substitution - we change one letter position (as in Caesar cipher)

Polygraphic substitution - we change more than one letter (pairs or larger groups of letters)

Monoalphabetic cipher - uses fixed substitution over the entire text. One good example is the Caesar cipher (much easier to decrypt)

Polyalphabetic cipher - uses a number of substitutions over the entire text. One good example is the **Playfair** cipher, the **Vigenere** cipher, and the **Jefferson wheel cipher** (much harder to decrypt)

Transposition

As the name implies, In a transposition algorithm, the plain text is reordered, we change the order of elements.

So if we have, for example, the word **"ATTACK NOW"**, and change the order. One way to do that (there are many ciphers, that use transposition), is to split the order of each letter

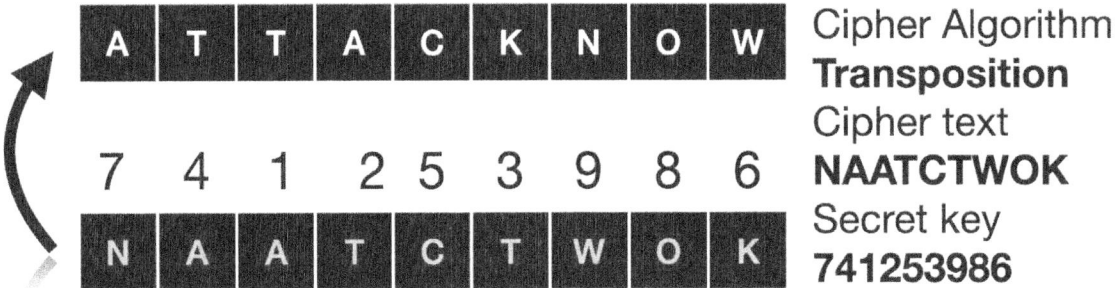

And we send the secret key, the secret key is the order.

So the order here is 741253986. We will rearrange the ciphertext according to the secret key

Caesar cipher

So let's move to our first classic cipher

The **Caesar cipher**.

A Caesar Cipher is a substitute cipher, we replace one word with another.

So the algorithm itself is "shift each letter in the alphabet"

The secret key is the number of times or the number of places.

In the following example, we use a basic cipher wheel, that you can create in your free time. It is composed of 2 parts, two alphabetic sets, one above the other

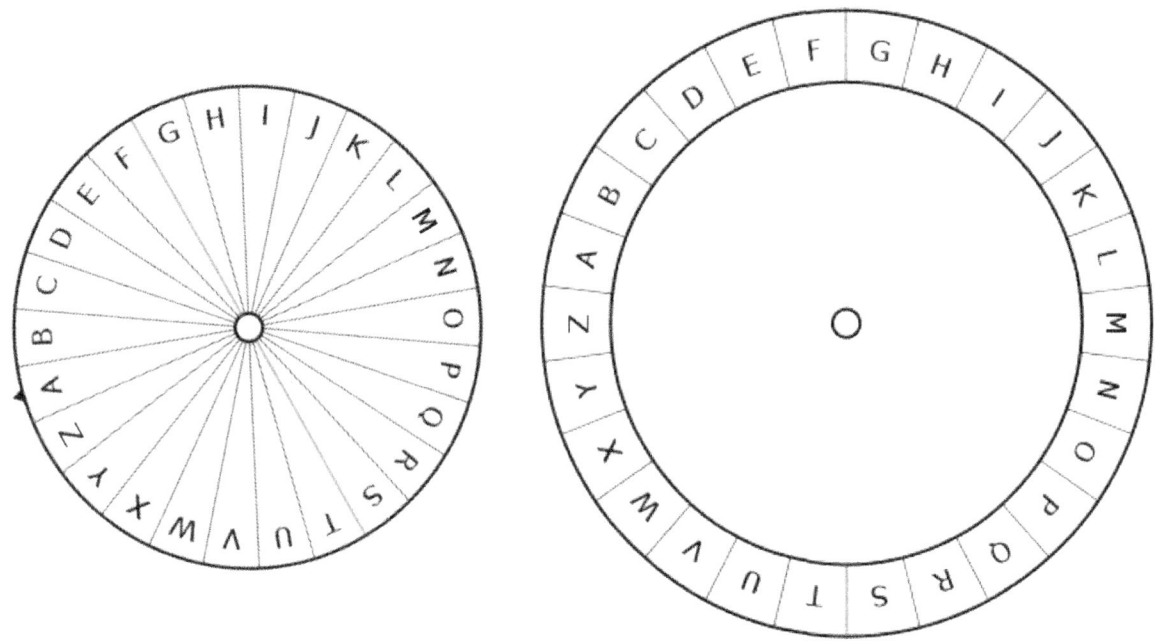

In the initial setup, each letter is aligned next to the other

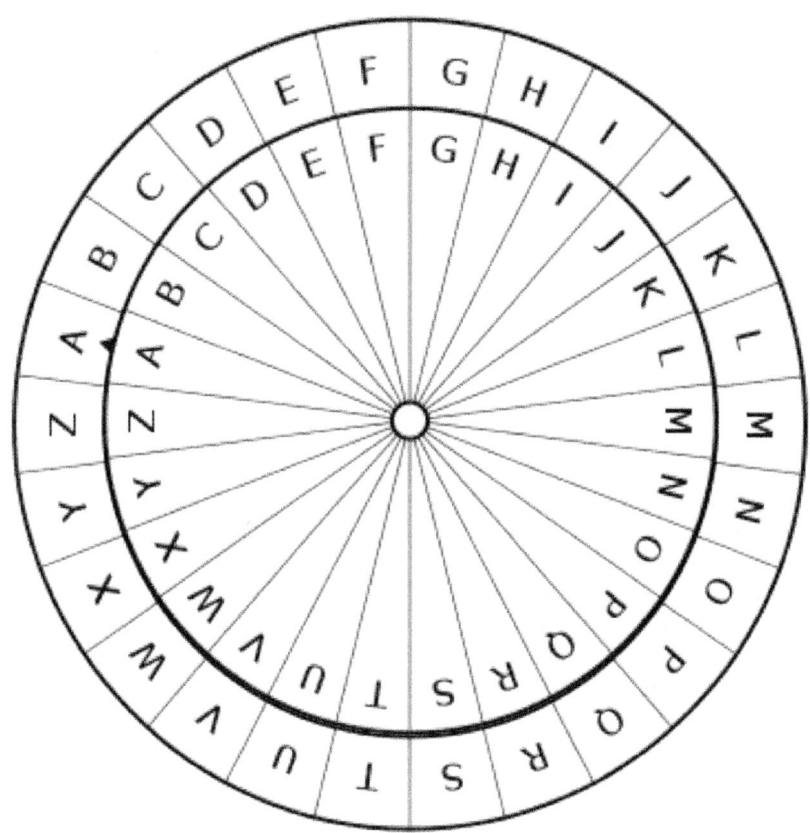

We decide that our secret key is 2

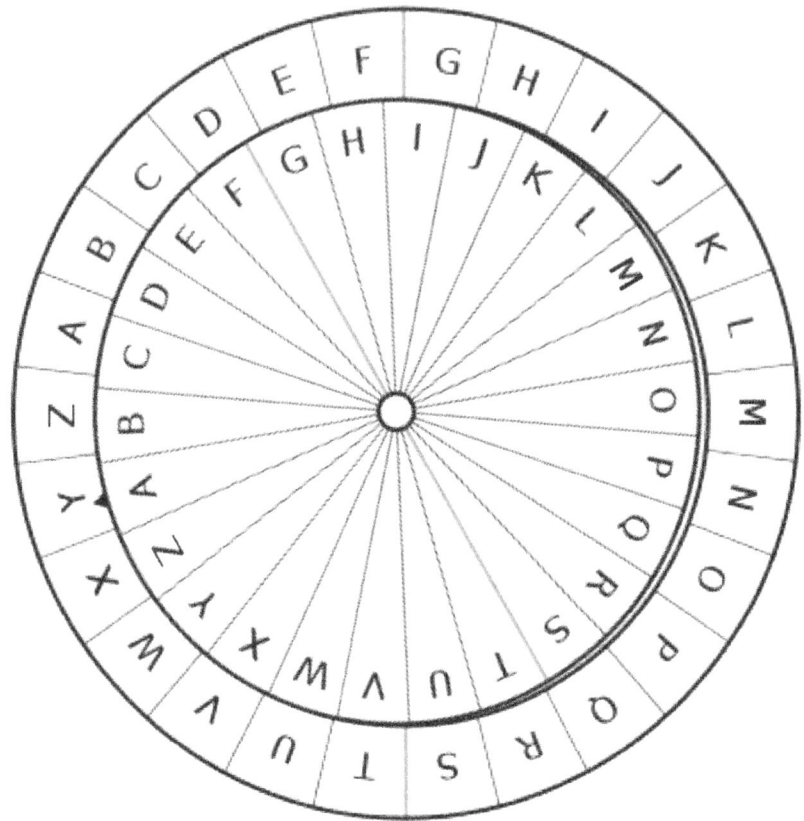

We can see the letter **A** becomes **C**, **T** becomes **V**, and so on.

Let's try to encrypt a plaintext, that says, **"Money"**. And our e secret key is **5**

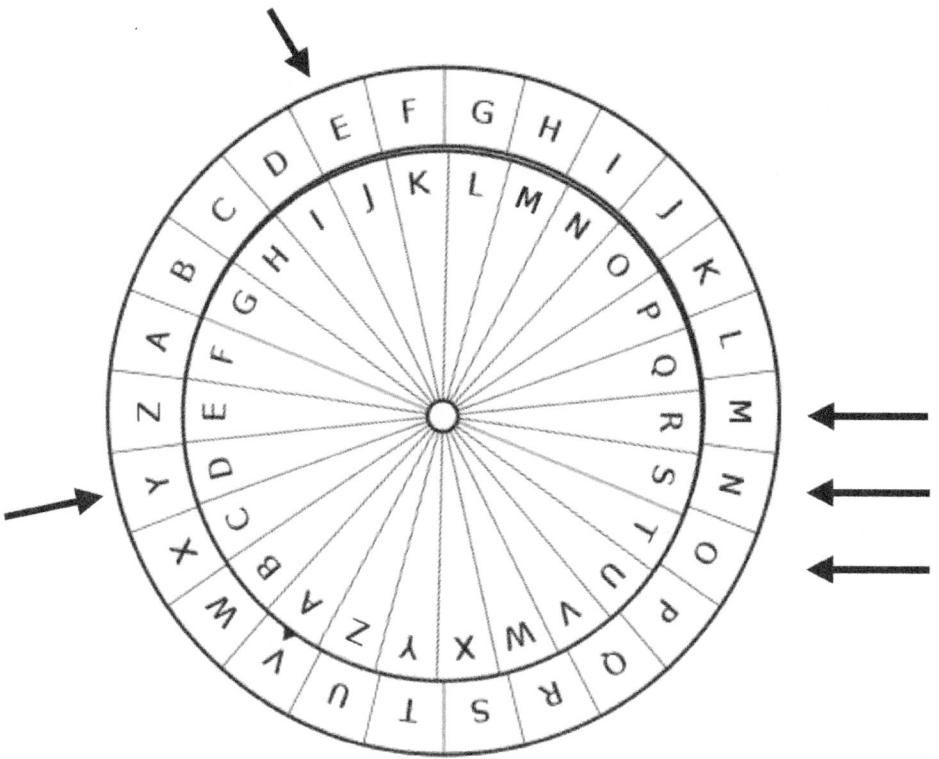

The keyspace is quite limited in Caesar cipher.

The English alphabet is only 26 characters, so we actually have only 26 possible keys, and a brute force attack (an attack that tries to guess the secret key) will be quite easy

A potential attacker will attempt to shift each letter one, place two places three places ahead, and finally, get the plain text.

A better way to improve our cipher is to use a polyalphabetic cipher as the **Vigenre cipher** which uses keywords (multiple substitution alphabets)

Another way that makes it, way harder, is to use the substitution of characters randomly, so our shift secret key will be a random number rather than a fixed one,

In that case, then we will have **26! (26 factorial)**

We use factorials to calculate how many permutations (different ways) we can arrange things

So If we have **n** different items (in our case 26), then we can arrange them in **n!**

26!

(**26** possibale values x **25** possible values x **24**....)

We have a keyspace of **403291461126605635584000000**

possibilities. if we translate this to a modern bit key system, then this is equivalent to a 2 to the power of 88 (2 times 2 times 2....)

2^{88}

You can play with **a factorial script** I wrote here:

https://repl.it/@ofershmueli/factorial-1#main.py

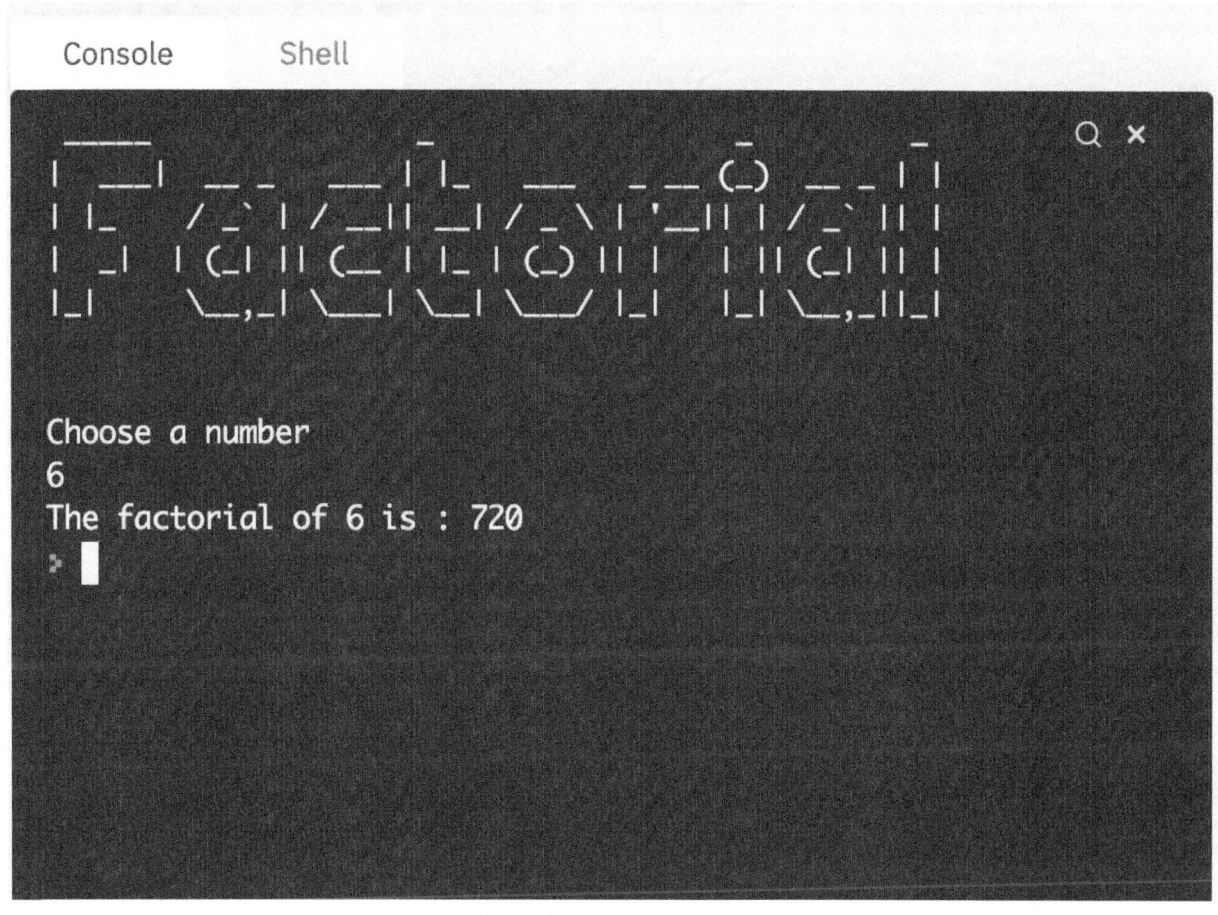

If we look back at our Plain text, let's imagine we need to cipher the message
"walking in the garden"

Plain text: walkinginthegarden

First Key: fghryteuwiopxmncb

First Key: fweudyrufhdkclxpxz.

The first letter **W** is replaced with the letter **F** is chosen randomly between the 26 possible characters.

The second letter, which is **A** turns out to be **W**. Why? Because it was randomly chosen. It wasn't chosen out of a pre-defined key.

You can use a keyspace that is almost impossible to crack if you're using randomness on the English alphabet.

Caesar Cipher was used 2000 years ago, they didn't use factorial 26, only 26 possible keys. Seems easy, right?

Well, it took more than **200 years** to break caesar cipher

Brute Force

Anyone who wishes to break the coded message, need to ask the following questions:

- How can we decrypt the ciphered message?
- How can we get the secret key?

When we use brute force attacks, we try all possible keys. When our cipher is with Caesar Cipher, there are only 26 possible keys. We will also look at other more sophisticated algorithms, that makes it much harder

But Nowadays, in our everyday life, we are using Binary Digits.

```
01100111 11111100 01111101 01111101 11011001 11001010 11101000 10011110 11101111 10100000 10010111 00100001 00010111 01000011 00011100
11100010 10011100 01100010 01011111 11010011 10001100 10001101 01110101 10010000 01011011 01110000 10111110 10110010 10110101 10011001
11001011 01001001 11100010 01011011 11000101 10001011 01000011 01000111 00011110 01001101 00000010 11100100 00011010 10010010 10000010
00100011 00011111 00001000 01011011 01001111 10100101 01111001 00111001 11001011 01101010 01000110 11101111 10010011 10000000 01100110
10111001 01010010 01100011 00000100 00001011 10011100 00101000 00010110 00111010 10000100 10011001 11010100 10001101 01100111 00000101
00100011 11010010 10000111 00011000 10011101 01111011 01010010 10001100 10101010 11101100 11100001 10100100 01001000 00101111 00100001
01000101 01010001 00100101 11110001 00110111 00100100 11010110 10101100 01011111 00110111 01100111 11111110 01111101 01111101 11011001
11001010 11101000 10011110 11101111 10100000 10010111 00100001 00010111 01000011 00011100 11100010 10011100 01100010 01011111 11010011
10001100 10001101 01110101 10010000 01011011 01110000 10111110 10110010 10110101 10011001 11001011 01001001 11100010 01011011 11000101
10001011 01000011 01000111 00011110 01001101 00000010 11100100 00011010 10010010 10000010 00100011 00011111 00001000 01011011 01001111
10100101 01111001 00111001 11001011 01101010 01000110 11101111 10010011 10000000 01100110 10111001 01010010 01100011 00000100 00001011
10011100 00101000 00010110 00111010 10000100 10011001 11010100 10001101 01100111 00000101 00100011 11010010 10000111 00011000 10011101
01111011 01010010 10001100 10101010 11101100 11100001 10100100 01001000 00101111 00100001 01000101 01010001 00100101 11110001 00110111
00100100 11010110 10101100 01011111 00110111 01100111 11111110 01111101 01111101 11011001 11001010 11101000 10011110 11101111 10100000
10010111 00100001 00010111 01000011 00011100 11100010 10011100 01100010 01011111 11010011 10001100 10001101 01110101 10010000 01011011
01110000 10111110 10110010 10110101 10011001 11001011 01001001 11100010 01011011 11000101 10001011 01000011 01000111 00011110 01001101
00000010 11100100 00011010 10010010 10000010 00100011 00011111 00001000 01011011 01001111 10100101 01111001 00111001 11001011 01101010
01000110 11101111 10010011 10000000 01100110 10111001 01010010 01100011 00000100 00001011 10011100 00101000 00010110 00111010 10000100
10011001 11010100 10001101 01100111 00000101 00100011 11010010 10000111 00011000 10011101 01111011 01010010 10001100 10101010 11101100
11100001 10100100 01001000 00101111 00100001 01000101 01010001 00100101 11110001 00110111 00100100 11010110 10101100 01011111 00110111
01100111 11111110 01111101 01111101 11011001 11001010 11101000 10011110 11101111 10100000 10010111 00100001 00010111 01000011 00011100
11100010 10011100 01100010 01011111 11010011 10001100 10001101 01110101 10010000 01011011 01110000 10111110 10110010 10110101 10011001
11001011 01001001 11100010 01011011 11000101 10001011 01000011 01000111 00011110 01001101 00000010 11100100 00011010 10010010 10000010
00100011 00011111 00001000 01011011 01001111 10100101 01111001 00111001 11001011 01101010 01000110 11101111 10010011 10000000 01100110
10111001 01010010 01100011 00000100 00001011 10011100 00101000 00010110 00111010 10000100 10011001 11010100 10001101 01100111 00000101
00100011 11010010 10000111 00011000 10011101 01111011 01010010 10001100 10101010 11101100 11100001 10100100 01001000 00101111 00100001
01000101 01010001 00100101 11110001 00110111 00100100 11010110 10101100 01011111 00111001
```

So when you hear of a **128-bit** key, that actually refers to **2** (our numbering base is binary, 0 and 1 in the digital world) to the power of 128

A brute force will almost take forever.

At the beginning of this book, we used a keypad with **0** to **9** digits, which is a base of **10** digits. we also used a **4** characters password, the keyspace was 10 to the power of 4, there were **10,000** possible values.

$$10^4$$

In the physical world, where you need to manually enter the password it is quite difficult to brute force and find the secret key

In the digital world, it is a matter of **milliseconds**.

Brute Force Table

Now, let's look at this table. And see how long does it take to brute force different keys (**find all possible keys in the keyspace**).

Our reference is a computer that is capable of a billion calculations in a second.

Key length	Key space	10^9/sec	10^{12}/sec	10^{15}/sec
32	2^{32}	4 sec		4 us
56	2^{56}	833 days		72 sec
64	2^{64}	584 yrs		
128	2^{128}	10^{22} yrs		
192	2^{192}	10^{41} yrs		10^{54} yrs

- If our keyspace is 2 to the power of 32, it will take him only **4** seconds.
- If our keyspace is 2 to the power 56 it will take him **833** days
- If our keyspace is 2 to the power 64 it will take him **584** years.

But take a look at what happens when we use a more modern keyspace.

128-bit key or **192-bit**

It will take an attacker, millions and billions of years. Making it impossible.

When we are using **2** to the power of **128** (which is the minimum keyspace used nowadays) a brute force attack is not feasible, unless an attacker has millions of years to test all combinations.

Every time we increase the length of the key by **1 bit**, we **double** the number of possible values

Bits, Permutations, and reversible Map

The following concept may be a bit confusing.

When we use a **2 Bit key**, we supposedly have only 4 values

When we encrypt using this 2bit key, we map the plain text to the ciphered text and vice versa. Encryption has to be reversible

Think of it as a table

Reversible Mapping

Plain text	Cipher text
00	11
01	10
10	00
11	01

But if we use permutations (Different ways that we can rearrange the bits). We can actually get 24 possible values, out of the four possible values, each value is a different combination or a different permutation of the different bits.

Key 1

Plain text	Cipher text
00	11
01	10
10	00
11	01

Key 2

Plain text	Cipher text
00	01
01	10
10	00
11	11

Key 3

Plain text	Cipher text
00	10
01	11
10	00
11	01

Key 4

Plain text	Cipher text
00	11
01	01
10	00
11	10

We use four keys, but you can get out of the two-bit key, 24 possible values. a factorial of four.

4!

We will send our recipient the number of the key we want him to use

Key 2

Plain text	Cipher text
00	01
01	10
10	00
11	11

Let's look at another example

If you're using a **3bit** key, which is 8 possible values

2^3

Factorial of 8 is more than 40,000 values. So if we're using permutation. We can create a mapping table that will lead to an enormous keyspace.

40,320

You can play with a bit key permutation using this small python script I wrote

https://repl.it/@ofershmueli/permutations-2#main.py

CryptAnalysis

Classic ciphers as Caesar cipher and others used different techniques to hide the original plain text.

Let's see what techniques were used to decrypt them and how crypt analysis works.

Cryptanalysis actually started in the eighth century, more than **1400 years** with the old Islam scholars.

They have found out that our texts have a very distinct **fingerprint.** Their findings are valid for most alphabets

Let's look at the English alphabet and the frequency of which characters appear throughout a regular plain text.

Letter	Percentage	Letter	Percentage
A	8.2	N	6.7
B	1.5	O	7.5
C	2.8	P	1.9
D	4.3	Q	0.1
E	12.7	R	6.0
F	2.2	S	6.3
G	2.0	T	9.1
H	6.1	U	2.8
I	7.0	V	1.0
J	0.2	W	2.4
K	0.8	X	0.2
L	4.0	Y	2.0
M	2.4	Z	0.1

We can see a repetition, in the English alphabet (26 characters):

The letter **E** appears more than **12%** throughout the text,

following that, the letter **T** appears more than **9%** in just about any regular text that is written

Moving on, the letter **A** more than **8%**.

So, even if you have a ciphertext, you can see that there are repeating characters (unigram) that appear more than others.

But it doesn't stop here...

When you look at a pair of letters **(bigrams)**, you can see that **ss, ee, ff** are much more common to see

ss	ee	tt	ff	ll	mm

When you look at one letter word, the word **A** and **I** are much more frequent than other one-letter words.

A	I

When you look at two letter words, the two that are more frequent than others are **"of", "to"...**

| of | to | in | it | is | as | at | so | we | he |

When you look at three-letter words, we find **"and"** and **"the"** that are much more frequent

| the | and |

And the last thing **H** frequently appears before the letter **E** as in the words **"he"**, **"then"** and **"the"**

| he | then | the |

Knowing all that, can you try to decrypt this ciphertext using the letter frequencies, as we have just learned?

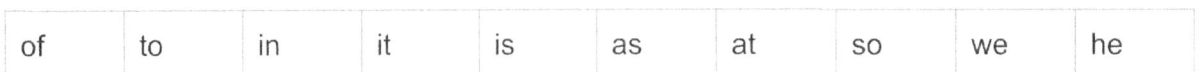

olssv lclyfvul dlsjvtl av aol lclua

If we look at the ciphertext, we can see that we have a bigram (two letters) **"SS"**

We can also see high frequent letters such as **L** that appears quite often (9 times, throughout the entire text)

And we can also see a two-letter word that appears here

So, let's see the plaintext...

Hello everyone welcome to the event

High frequency individual Letters, Pairs and 2 letter words

And the plaintext is **"Hello everyone, welcome to the event"**

We can see that the letter **"e"** is used frequently in our text

we can also see **"th"** and we as a Bigram, And we can see the two-letter word **"to"**.

If we have frequent usages of specific letters, such as **"e", "t", "a"**, and other letters, we can actually decrypt the ciphertext.

You can use a small python script that I wrote, to check out the frequency of letters

https://repl.it/@ofershmueli/letter-frequency#main.py

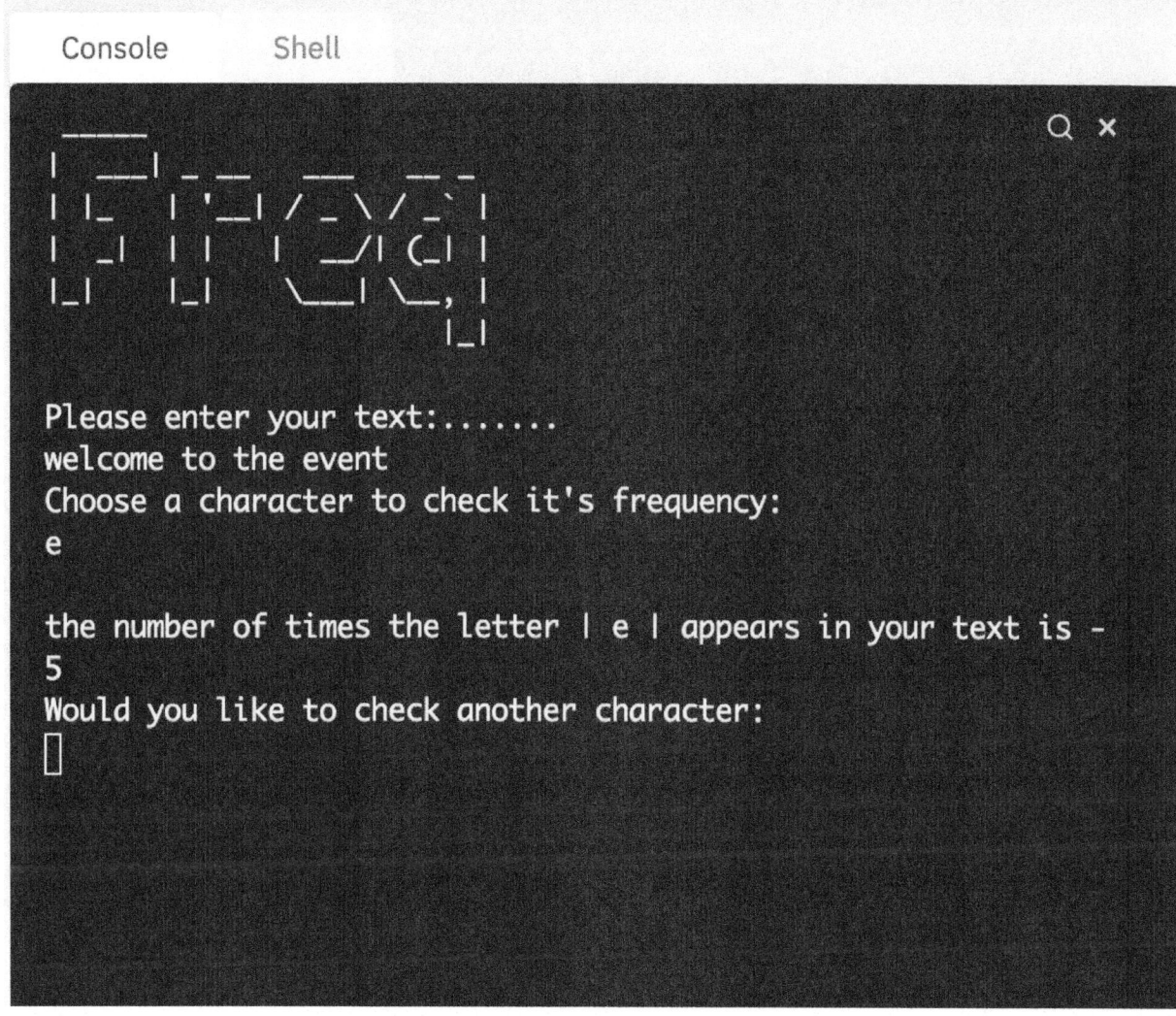

How do we overcome frequency analysis?

There are several techniques.

The first one is to delete spaces between the different words.

The second technique is to use similar letters, for example, **"S"** instead of **"Z"**.

But the best technique is just to use another algorithm that is more immune to frequency analysis. one is the **Playfair cipher**.

Playfair Cipher

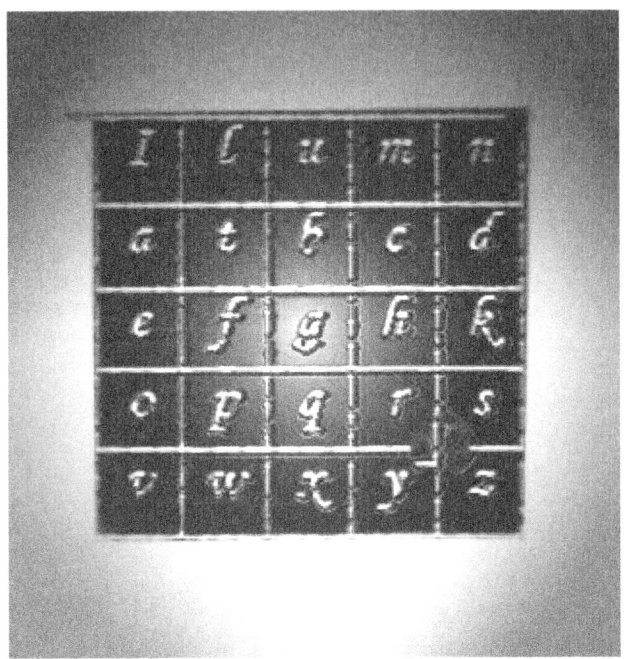

Playfair cipher was used throughout the 19th century. I actually heard of it, 15 years ago, when I saw the movie **"national treasure book of secrets"**

The Playfair cipher is a **digraph substitution cipher,** it uses pairs of letters (bigram) instead of single letters as in Caesar cipher

In the Playfair cipher, we use letter pairs (bigram) and a 5x5 matrix

5x5 matrix

Another thing, that we need, is a keyword, one that both parties know about.

t	h	a	i	l
n	d	b	c	e
f	g	k	m	o
p	q	r	s	u
v	w	x	y	z

keyword - Thailand

The encryption process goes like that...

let's assume that our keyword, the secret is, that's the word **"Thailand"**. it will be our **secret key.**

We start to fill our matrix, with our keyword **"Thailand"**

And then we start the alphabet. Whenever there's a character that already appears in the word **"Thailand"**, we skip it, so our first letter is **"b"** since we already have the letter **"a"**, in "Thailand"

Followed by **"c"** and then **"e"** since **"d"** already appears in our keyword. Now, let's assume that we wish to encrypt the word **"transportation"**

As said, the Playfair cipher involves letter pairs.

So let's start with the **"T"** and **"R"**, the first pair in the word **"transportation"**

t	h	a	i	l
n	d	b	c	e
f	g	k	m	o
p	q	r	s	u
v	w	x	y	z

look for the specific letters that you need to encrypt on your matrix.

To encrypt our pair (**T** and **R**) we will look at the same row and column that the letters appear in.

And there we find the letters **A** and **P**

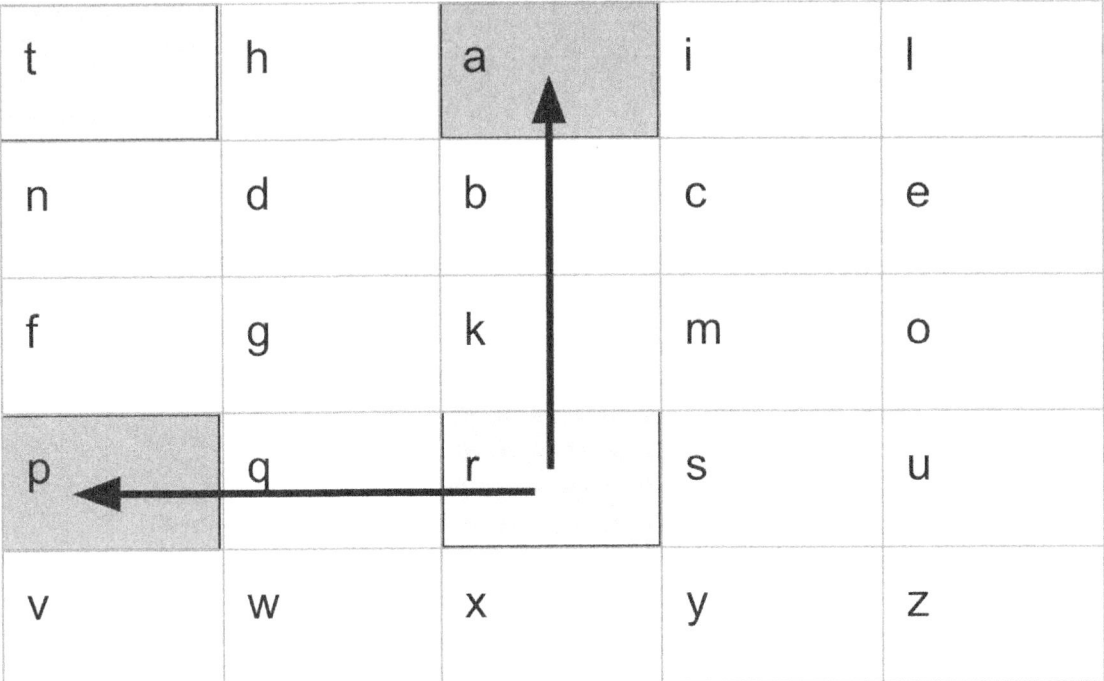

P and **R** will become the first 2 encrypted letters.

T becomes **A** and **R** becomes **P**

Let's continue. The next pair is "**A**" and "**N**".

if we look at the same row and column, we can see that we have the letters B, and the letter T.

t	h	a	i	l
n	d	b	c	e
f	g	k	m	o
p	q	r	s	u
v	w	x	y	z

t	h	a	i	l
n	d	b	c	e
f	g	k	m	o
p	q	r	s	u
v	w	x	y	z

So the letter **"B"** and **"T"** becomes the cipher letters for that digraph

AN = BT
Plain text **Cipher** text

We continue up until we encrypt the whole message.

The Playfair cipher is also known as a square cipher, it also uses substitution in order to encrypt the message itself. Although it does so with letter pairs which make it harder to decrypt

Our next cipher is way harder to decrypt, it is a polyalphabetic cipher, that uses substitution, but the difference is that it does so, using multiple substitute alphabets, so the relations between the single plain text letter to the encrypted one is **"one to many "**

Vigenere cipher

Vigenere **cipher** is one of my favorites. The technique it uses is very interesting

The Vigenere cipher was first described in 1553, it wasn't broken up until 300 years later

In Vigenere cipher, you are not limited to one fixed substitute or a letter pair. You need to choose a keyword that will serve as the secret key
 As always, both parties need to know the keyword

Vigenere cipher works on substitute operation techniques. So if we have a plain text **" Hi, everyone, welcome."** And our keyword is "golden". We use the word Goldman time after time repeatedly, just under the original plain text letters

 **keyword**=goldman

How do we use substitution?

We look at the keyword, the first letter is **G**.

G is number 6 in the English alphabet (we start our count when A is = 0 and B = 1…).

We move the letter H (original Plain text letter), 6 places

Key- goldmangoldmango
Plain text- hieveryonewelcome

Cipher- nwpyqrlubpzqlpuap

Shift the "h" letter "g" (6) places

And so on . with every letter, we look at its position in the alphabet, and we shift the original letter.

In the end, we have a **ciphertext**.

To decrypt vigenere code fast, you will need an Encryption Table That will help you to shift letters easily

So if our message is: **"sendhelp"** and our key is **"bulgebul"** we need to shift each letter according to its number

original message- "sendhelp"
original message- "bulgebul"

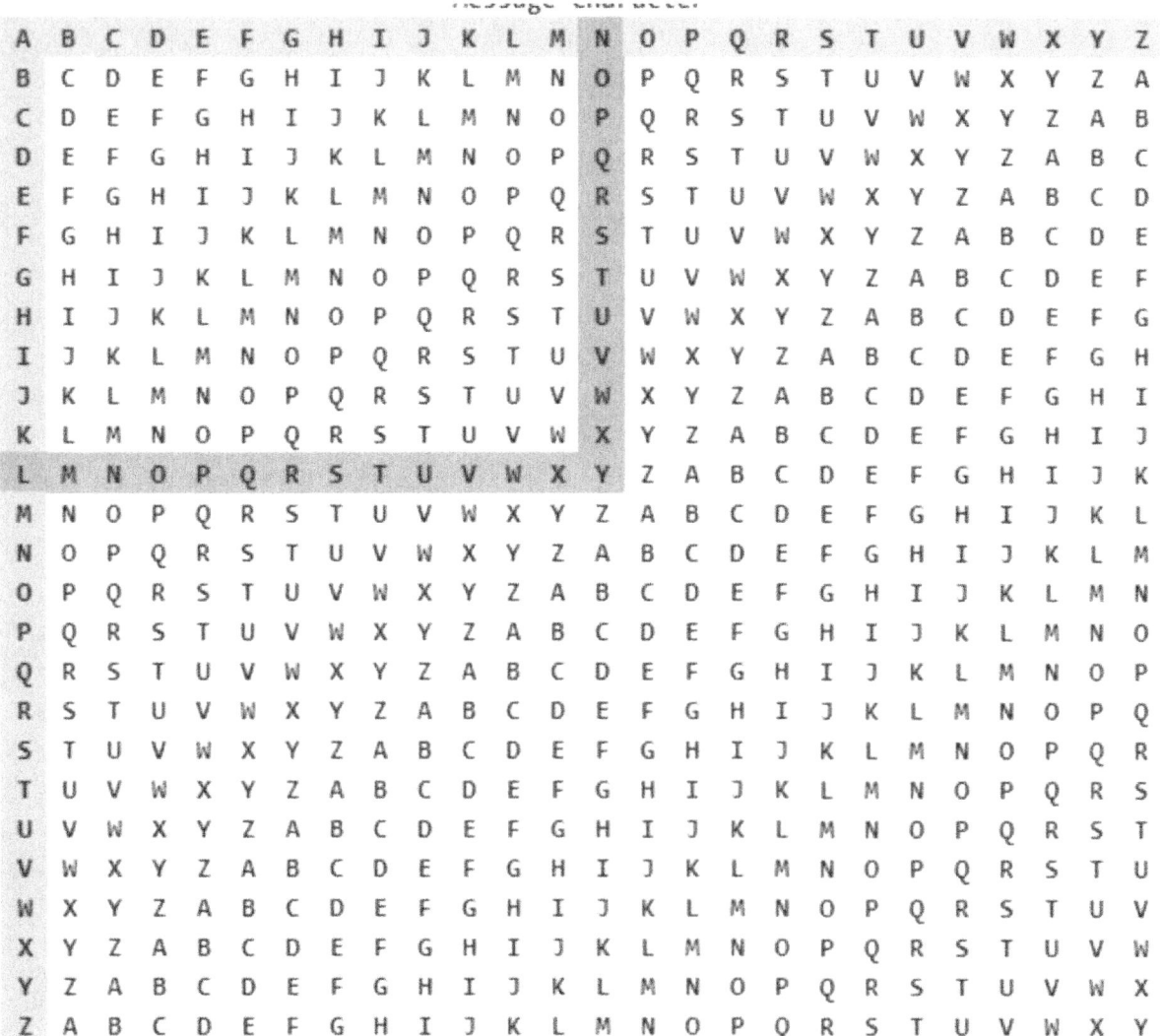

https://commons.wikimedia.org/wiki/File:Vigenere_Field_Table.png

Using the table, we can easily calculate it, in our example, the letter **"N"** is shifted **"L"** places, to become **"y"**

Breaking Vigenere Cipher

Knowing the length of your key will make it very easy to find the repetition in the text and decrypt the code

If you can find the key length (the keyword length) and if the keyword is not just a random set of characters, but a common word, then breaking the code becomes something that is realistic

Autokey **Cipher**

Another version of the Vigenere cipher was introduced later in the 16th century, the **AutoKey Cipher** that added, one more obstacle. A keyword + the text of the original plain text, that were added to the keyword

Plain Text — attackatdawn
key — summer

summerattackatd…
―――――――――――
attackatdawn

Autokey cipher

You can play around with random keywords using my python script here

https://repl.it/@ofershmueli/Random-keywords#main.py

To conclude this part of our crypto book, a good algorithm makes the letter **appear random**, with no frequency at all. Vigenere cipher was a very good polyalphabetic cipher for his time, it used multiple substitutions, and yet it wasn't perfect enough as the keyword repeated itself

The perfect cipher, with full randomness, is the one-time pad

Transposition Ciphers

Substitution is used heavily on encryption algorithms, the other technique is the transposition

Using Transposition, we re-order our plain text units (usually letters) . the result is a permutation.
Let's look at some examples

Columnar transposition cipher

A very basic transposition cipher is the Columnar cipher. here we will reorder the plain text in a table. letters are written horizontally and the ciphertext is read vertically

Our Plain Text is "attack at dawn"
We will use a table of 3 columns and 3 rows

a	k	w
t	a	n
t	t	
a	d	
c	a	

Our ciphertext is read vertically

a	k	w
t	a	n
t	t	
a	d	
c	a	

Cipher Text:**"akwtanttadca"**

The recipient of this message needs to know that the table is 3x3

In the same way, we can encrypt our message, with 2 columns and 6 rows

a	a
t	t
t	d
a	a
c	w
k	n

Our Ciphertext is read in a zig-zag manner

a	a
t	t
t	d
a	a
c	w
k	n

Ciphertext : **"aatttdaacwkn"**

You can make the columnar cipher much harder to decrypt, using a secret key

t	h	e	a	t
t	a	c	k	w
i	l	l	s	t
a	r	t	t	o
d	a	y		

Our secret message is **" the attack will start today "**

We will use a 5x5 table, writing the message vertically

Along with the table size, we will also send the other side a secret key **"31524"**

The cipher text is "hairaakstttiad….

3	1	5	2	4
t	h	e	a	t
t	a	c	k	w
i	l	l	s	t
a	r	t	t	o
d	a	y		

Using the secret key, the recipient will know how to position the ciphered letters in the table and find the plain text

Jefferson cipher wheel

Rendering of the wheelcipher - Wikipedia

The U.S president **Thomas Jefferson** was known for his curiosity and interest in the art of cryptography. his most famous crypto invention was the **cipher wheel**, which he didn't believe at first that is secure enough, and actually choose another cryptosystem over it although, his own system was far more secure

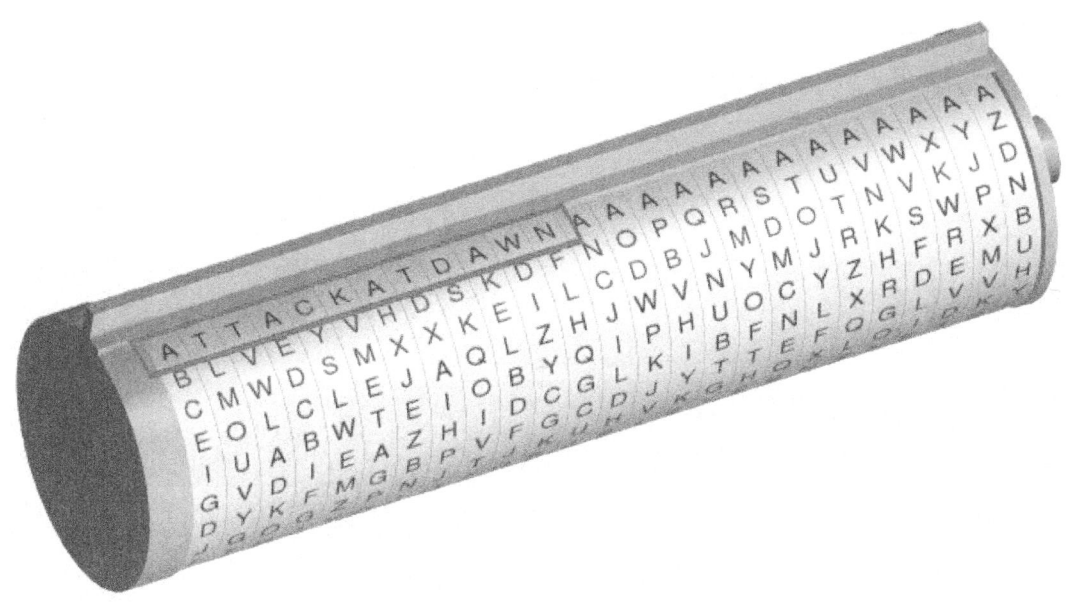

Jefferson has actually created a polyalphabetic cipher, that uses multiple substitutions of the English alphabet

He used 36 disk wheels, each disk had the English alphabet printed on it, each with a different permutation (random order)

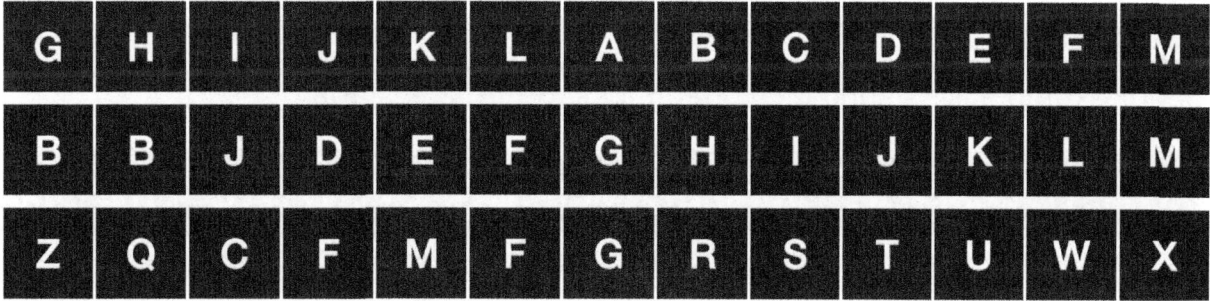

The second one had another random order
And then the third one, and so on

The 36 disks were inserted into a cylinder type apparatus one after the other, But, in an order that only the two sides knew (the sender and the recipient)

So for example, if our ordered disks look like that :

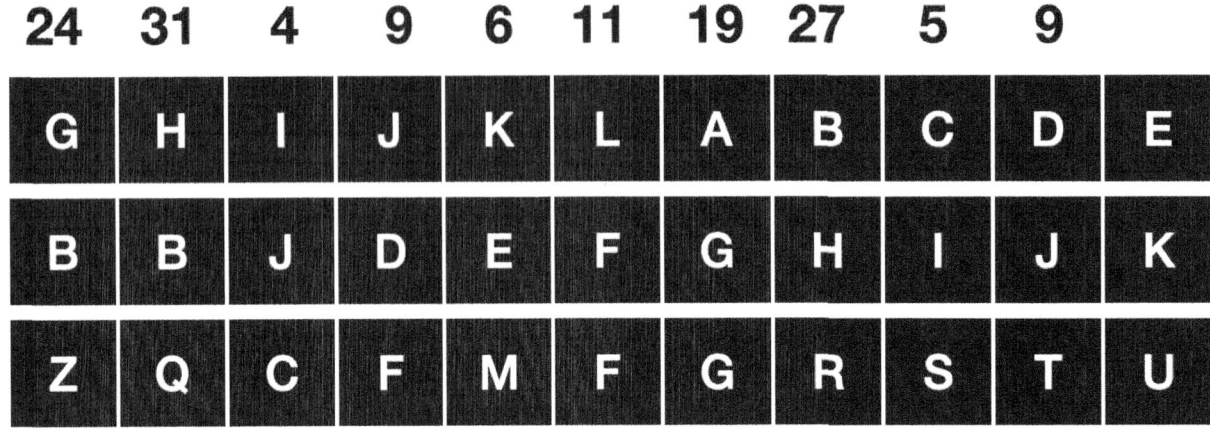

Disk number 24, will be inserted first into the cylinder, followed by disk 31, 4….

This type of permutation leads to an enormous keyspace

To write the encrypted message, the sender orders the disks and aligns the letters to make a line that is readable

So for example, let's send the coded message "Attack starts "

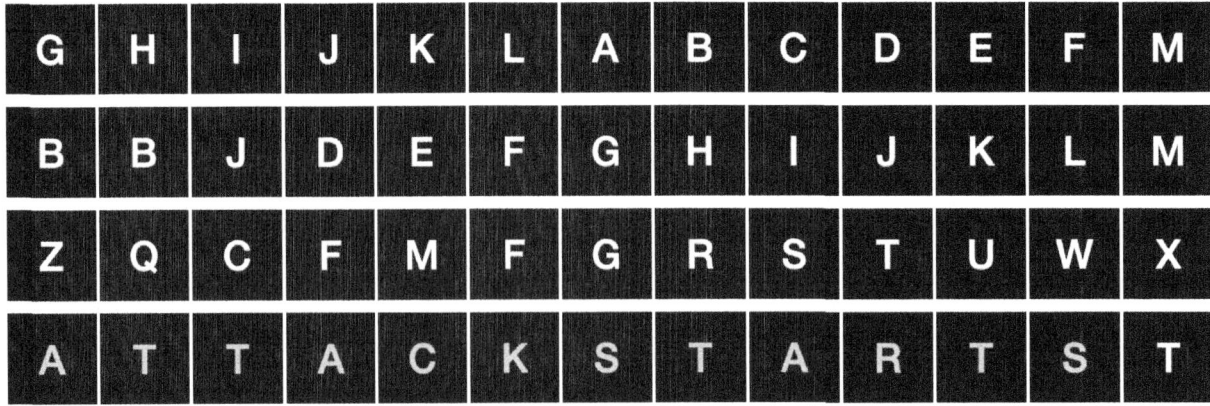

And then look to any other line of text (for the sake of our example, let's assume, that the sender chooses another line, which is shifted 3 places above) and copies the rest of the letters from that line into the paper

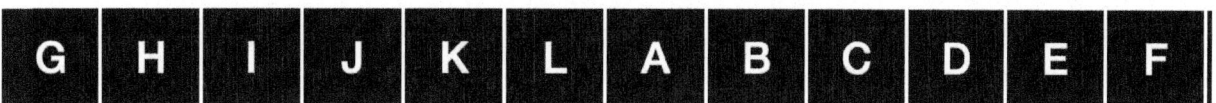

We get a coded message, random letters, with no meaning

The coded message is sent to the recipient
He will arrange the coded letters, one after the other, following the order of the disks, and then will look for lines of letters that make out sensible words

Jefferson Wheel keyspace = 36! (36x35x34x33.....)

Thomas Jefferson has actually succeeded in calculating the keyspace as 372 followed by 39 zeroes. if we calculate it using binary, then this is a 138-bit key

$$2^{138}$$

One-Time Pad

```
CIHJT UUHML FRUGC ZIBGD BQPNI PDNJG LPLLP YJYXM
DCXAC JSJUK BIOYT MWQPX DLIRC BEXYK VKIMB TYIPE
UOLYQ OKOXH PIJKY DRDBC GEFZG UACKD RARCD HBYRI
DZJYO YKAIE LIUYW DFOHU IOHZV SRNDD KPSSO JMPQT
MHQHL OHQQD SMHNP HHOHQ GXRPJ XBXIP LLZAA VCMOG
AWSSZ YMFNI ATMON IXPBY FOZLE CVYSJ XZGPU CTFQY
HOVHU OCJGU QMWQY OIGOR BFHIZ TYFDB VBRMN XNLZC
```

The idea is simple: ciphertext should provide no clue about the plain text

The **one-time pad** is a polyalphabetic cipher that uses random characters as long as the message continues. This way, no fingerprints, or frequent letters could be analyzed. To ensure perfect secrecy, the key is only used once (that's why it is called a one time pad)

Imagine, that you have to send a letter, 1000 characters long. for each character in your plain text, you will use randomly generated characters, each with its own shift, with no repetition whatsoever

The Random key in the one-time pad is long as the plain text

Used correctly, One-Time Pad is an **unbreakable cipher**

Throughout the Cold War, we have seen the usage of a one-time pad, but it was only used for short messages.

The key in a one-time pad is only used once each character is randomly chosen.

There are no frequent letters and the text looks random.

Imagine that you have a twenty-six-**sided** dice

On each side, a letter from the alphabet

You roll the dice and choose one letter

This is as close as you can come close to real randomness

Plain Text

wewillattacktommorow

One Time Pad **Random** Encryption Key

ashjuixcvdfgnntknbfywi

Cipher Text

WWDRFTXVODHQOLMYZNTPKE

For each letter in our plain text, you roll the dice and shift the original letter, X places according to the result

Results could be different if used with another key

But it is not practical. for 2 main reasons:

- Key distribution- Delivering the key to both sides is challenging, so is used mainly for short messages
- Generating a truly random key is challenging

True Random

Randomness is key to a good secret key. If it's used in a one-time pad, there is no frequency whatsoever, but randomness is hard to get. Where do we get randomness? in nature as in Atmospheric events, but that is not feasible for our needs, so we generate pseudo-random numbers using computer algorithms, which we will look at in the next chapter

Moving to **Binary**

When we try to generate random numbers using our computers, we actually generate a pseudo-random number since our computers are actually machines with instructions behind them.

Up until now, we have played with letters, but we are not working with letters anymore. We are working with a binary digit **(bit)**, everything is being translated into a 1, and a 0 **(1 and 0 are used on our computers, so the base is always 2 to the power of the number of elements in the bit string)**.

When using bits, the key length is a string of bits, the keyspace is actually, the number of bits in the key

So if for example, we have a key that is **01011010** :

$$2^8$$

The keyspace is 2 to the power of 8, which is 256 possible keys (1 and 0 can be represented in this key in 256 different patterns.

Remember, every bit that is added to our key, doubles the keyspace, a 2 to the power of 9, is 512 possible keys

So now we can look at that as plain binary digits. and a secret key made of the bit string

Plain Binary

0111010100101010101010

One Time Pad Encryption Key

110101010100100011111

And our algorithm takes the two parts, the plain Binary and the Binary Key And it does binary math, known also as BitWise operations on every single Bit

One of the BitWise operators, that are used heavily in cryptography is **XOR** (exclusive OR)

XOR is a logic operation, used frequently in many Apps, it compares 2 Bit inputs and generates one Bit Input

The Logic behind XOR is very simple:
- If the bits are different, then the result is **1**
- If the bits are the same, then the result is **0**

Bit 1	Bit 2	XOR
0	0	0
0	1	1
1	0	1
1	1	0

The encrypted text is the text that is being XORed.
If you want to reverse and get back your plain message, you take the ciphertext, you take the key, and you do the same sort of operation.

Plain Text
00100101010010010010

One Time Pad **Random** Encryption Key
11010100100000010101

Cipher Text Using XOR operation
11110001110010000111

In the modern era, Bits are used to represent everything

If our plain text message is " **this is a secret key** "

```
  GNU nano 2.0.6              File: text                    Modified

this is a secret key
```

This is how it is represented in Bits using the XXD tool on my Mac terminal

```
ofers-MBP:~ ofer$ xxd -b text
```

```
ofers-MBP:~ ofer$ xxd -b text
00000000: 01110100 01101000 01101001 01110011 00100000 01101001  this i
00000006: 01110011 00100000 01100001 00100000 01110011 01100101  s a se
0000000c: 01100011 01110010 01100101 01110100 00100000 01101011  cret k
00000012: 01100101 01111001 00100000 00001010                    ey .
ofers-MBP:~ ofer$
```

A one-time-pad that will be used to encrypt that plain text, should be at least at the same size

Message Length=**Key** Length

Random Numbers

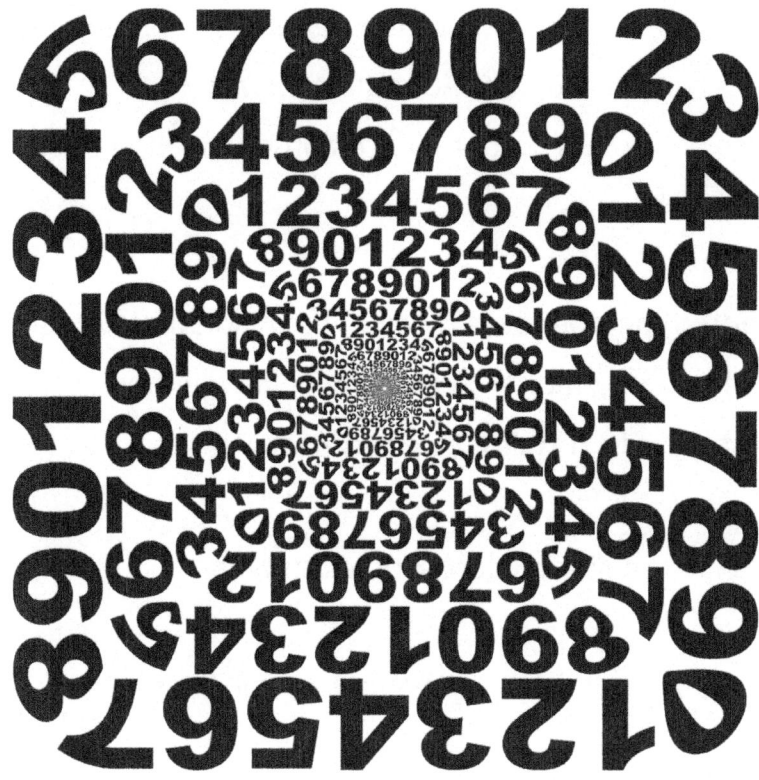

Random numbers are used everywhere in modern cryptography. keys which are nothing more than bitstrings should be unpredictable and are generated fast and every time we make an encrypted connection on the internet.

Entropy

To Understand random numbers, let's look at another very important term **"Entropy"**

The term was used already in the 19th century, but for the sake of this book and our subject, which is cryptography, we will look at Information Entropy as invented by Claude Shannon, one of the fathers of modern communication back in 1948

We can look at entropy, from different perspectives, but the definition that I would use, for our topic, is "the measure of predictability", how difficult it would be to predict the number, **a higher entropy is harder to predict**

We measure entropy in Bits. let's look at some interesting examples

A coin toss, has an entropy of **1bit**, since, it can only have **2** possibilities

In The next example, we will look at our computer/smartphones password, How random, or how difficult it is to predict your password or to brute force, it using different attack techniques

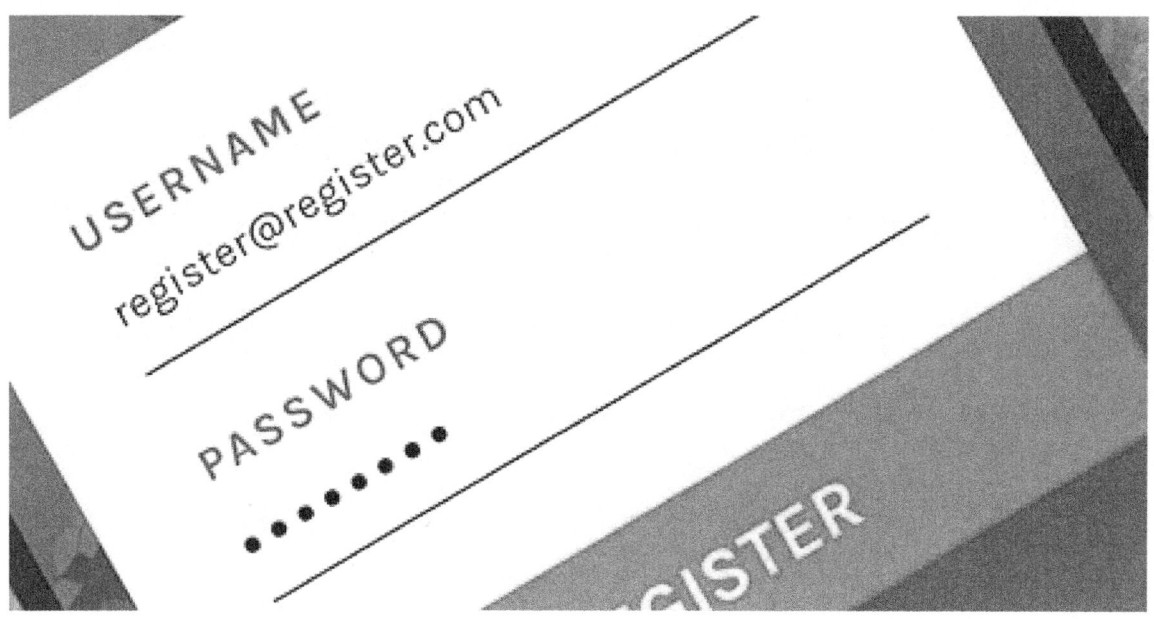

How do We calculate Our **Password Entropy**?

We can calculate our password entropy, using the different attributes it has:
- The length of your password
- The complexity of your password
- Are you using uppercase characters, lowercase, or maybe both
- Are you using symbols? Are you using numbers?

The more complex your password is there is much more entropy !!!

And the last parameter is the…. You guessed it, the Randomness of your password. The more random it is, it adds up more entropy

The entropy formula is as follows.

$$H = L * \log_2(N)$$

H is the total binary bits of entropy (remember that entropy is measured in bits) is located using bits.

L is the length of your password

N is the number of possible symbols in your passwords

SO, For example, if we use a password of 8 characters length, but the complexity is all 94 characters and symbols on our keyboard (upper and lower case letters, numbers, symbols..)

The amount of password possibilities (very similar to the exercise we made at the beginning of the book is :

$$94^8$$

94 is our base (**complexity**), and 8 is our **key length**

But, we use Bits in entropy, so that would come out as :

$$2^{52}$$

This password has 52 bits of entropy. it is a strong password, the higher your password entropy, the less predictable, your password patterns are for a hacker.

Here are some more examples:

Upper/Lower case Symbols and Digits	Bits	Passwords
6	39.2	689 billion
7	45.8	64.8 trillion
12	78.6	475 Sextillion

True And **Pseudo**

We divide random numbers into 3 groups :
- True
- Psuedo random
- Hybrid

True **Random**

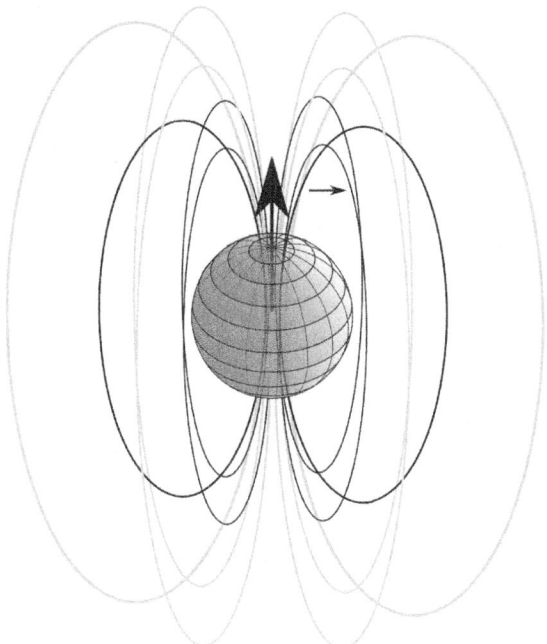

True random numbers are very hard to collect and for most cases, the period of such phenomena is also too short. we see real randomness in electromagnetic phenomena, in atmospheric events where the attributes are constantly changing and are impossible to predict

Pseudo-**Random**

$$X_{n+1} = (aX_n + b) \bmod m$$

When we deal with pseudo-random keys (mostly in computers), we use algorithms, the operation starts with a seed number, which can be thought of as our random number initial value. This number is used by the algorithm to generate the pseudo-random number key. It looks random, but it is actually deterministic

Psuedo number generator use different operations through a mathematical equation, where it increment , subtracts , uses factorial operations

2,7,9,44,1,333,2,5,6,77,8,8,99,34,44…..

If an attacker knows the seed value, the full random sequence can be reproduced

Random numbers generator should be fast

Hybrid Random **Numbers**

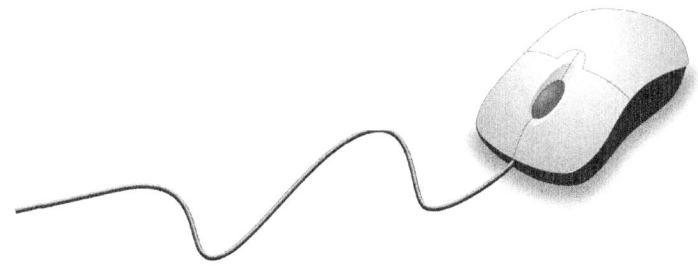

To generate a hard unpredictable random number, we use other sources (physical events) to make the entropy (ability to predict) harder such as :
- The time that we started to generate our numbers i.e 02:33
- keyboard presses
- Mouse movement
- Computer fan operation

The data that it takes from the physical operations adds up to the randomness of the key

Your Own **Algorithm**

You can actually generate your own random number sequence, using the following method, known as the **Middle Square** method. It is by no means secure, but it's a nice practice in generating short and simple random numbers

You start with a 2 digit initial value (seed) - for our demonstration, we will use the number **22**

Square that number

The result is:

484

If you get a - 3 digit number result, add 0 to left

0484

Pick the middle 2 digits (48) and discard the rest

So our first random number in the sequence is 48

Next, square the number 48

48^2

The result is:

2304

Again pick the 2 middle numbers, ignore the rest

Your second number in the sequence is 30

And again square the number 30 ….

In the end, you should get a sequence like that

SEED = 22

Random Numbers
48
30
90
10

You can use the Mid Square algorithm, with an initial 4 digit number, and then, you square the number, pick the middle 4 digits (if you get a- 7 number digit result, just add a - 0 before and continue with the operation)

Up until now, we have looked at the classical ciphers, Caesar Cipher, Playfair cipher, Vigenere, columnar ciphers, and even the Jefferson cipher wheel. There are dozens more but they seem to best represent the algorithms operation's

We have also looked at cryptanalysis, how do we use the letter frequency, either single letter unit, pairs, one letter words, analyzing their frequency helps to decrypt the cipher

In modern life, our secret key moves through different rooms, where it is being shifted, transposition, cuts by half ....and then at the end XORed with the original plain text. The Tales that a secret key goes through is unbelievable

Now it is time for some advanced techniques that are used today

We will look at **Symmetric Encryption**

Symmetric Encryption

We move on to the modern era, where we use binary data instead of plain letters

As with the ciphers from the classical era, modern Symmetric ciphers also use the same key to encrypt and decrypt.

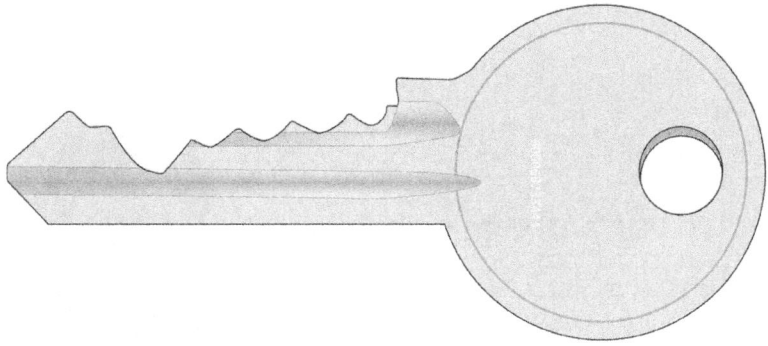

We divide between two variants of symmetric ciphers:
The first one is a **block cipher**
The second one is a **stream cipher**.
The main difference between them is the amount of data that each algorithm encrypts.

Stream Cipher

A stream cipher usually encrypts a bit or one byte of data. It encrypts only small chunks of data.

It is much faster than a block cipher. (Though in today's hardware that is barely noticeable) Let's take a use case which is a voice-over IP call or any other real-time application.

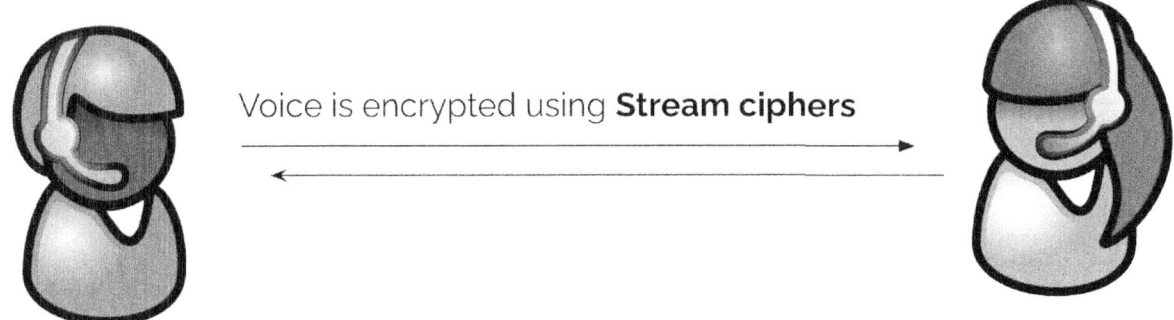

Both parties hold the same key which is used to decrypt the data.

When we speak our analog voice turns into a binary bitstream, and it is being sent to the other side

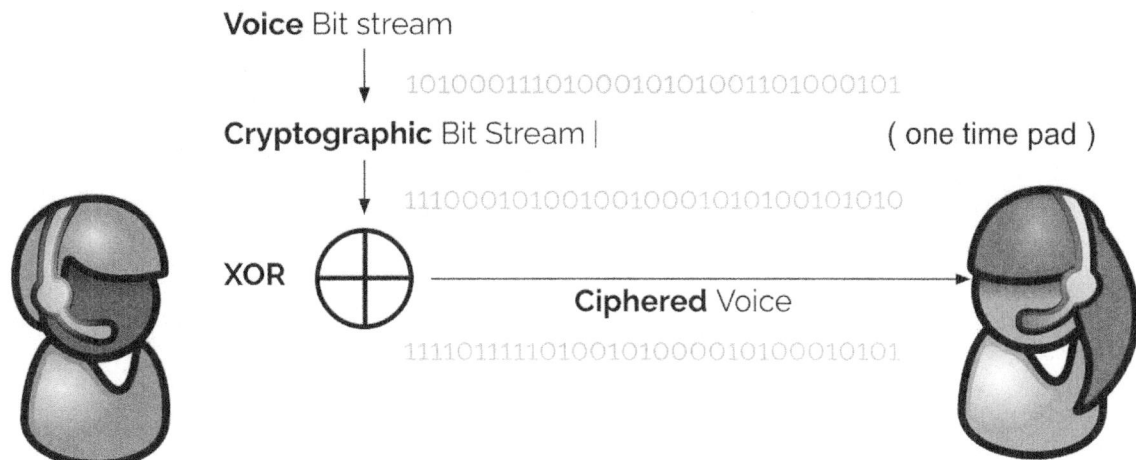

In this example we can see:

- The voice Bitstream
- the cryptographic Key (let us imagine that it is a one-time-pad)
- Our algorithm takes the two inputs and does the XOR operation

The output is a **ciphered voice**

On the other side, we have the same key. We receive a bitstream of the cipher voice. And now we can use the same XOR operation with the key to turning the cipher voice into the original plain bitstream

Encrypting **Text**

Another example is the encryption of a plain text
The word is **"attack"**, and the first thing we will do, is to convert it to binary data, for that we will use the ASCII character set, as used in our computers, each letter is converted into an 8 bit **(Byte)** string

ASCII Code

Now let's use our binary data and XOR the plain text with the key

Plain Text	01100001 01110100 01110100 01100001 01100011 01101011	
Key	00010001 11010100 01000100 01111001 01000000 00101001	⊕ XOR

And the result is our **Ciphered text**

To decrypt our ciphertext, we will use the XOR operation on our ciphertext and the Key

Cipher text	11100001 01000000 01100000 00110000 0100011 01000010	
Key	00010001 11010100 01000100 01111001 01000000 00101001	⊕ XOR
Plain Text	01100001 01110100 01110100 01100001 01100011 01101011	

Block cipher

Block cipher on the other side encrypts groups of bits, known as Blocks (64, 128...Bit).

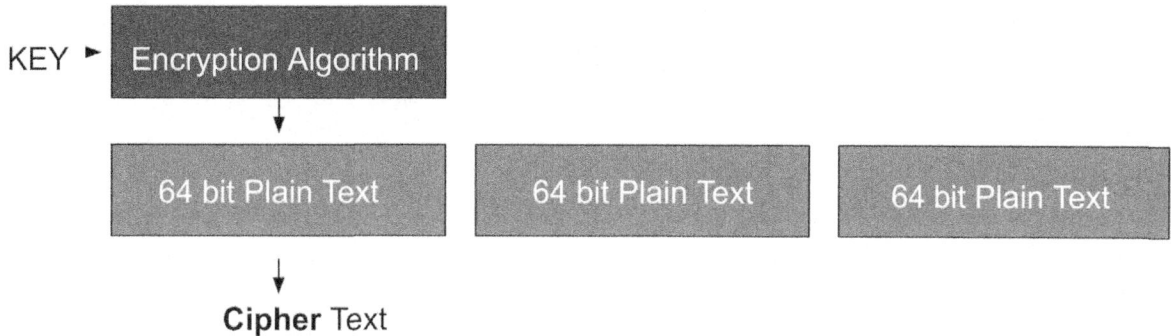

If we will look back at the "attack" text example, our block cipher will encrypt chunks of text as one block, followed by the other

attack

01100001 01110100 01110100 01100001 01100011 01101011

Block of bits

Among the Known Block ciphers that are used or were used for years are **AES, BlowFish,** and **DES**

Block Ciphers are slower than stream ciphers only due to the fact that it encrypts bigger chunks. but in today's hardware, it is not an issue.

What happens when it finishes encrypting the different blocks?

It needs to aggregate them.

It does so using **"modes of operation"**

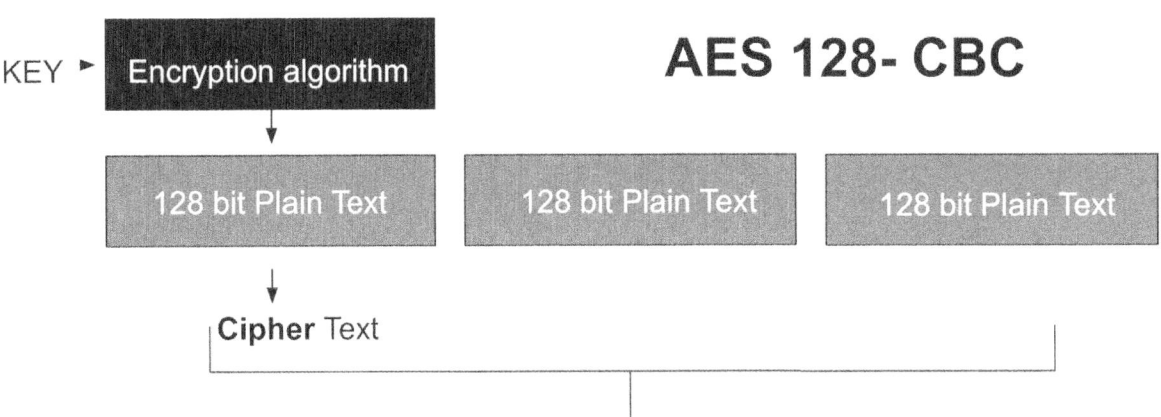

There are different modes of operation in block ciphers as **CBC** (Cipher Block Chaining), **ECB** (Electronic Code Book) and there are others

Ciphers work on a fixed block unit, so when we encrypt using **AES128**, we encrypt 128 bits of data, at the end of the file, it joins them all together. But what happens, if the last part of our file is not 64 bits or 128 bits.

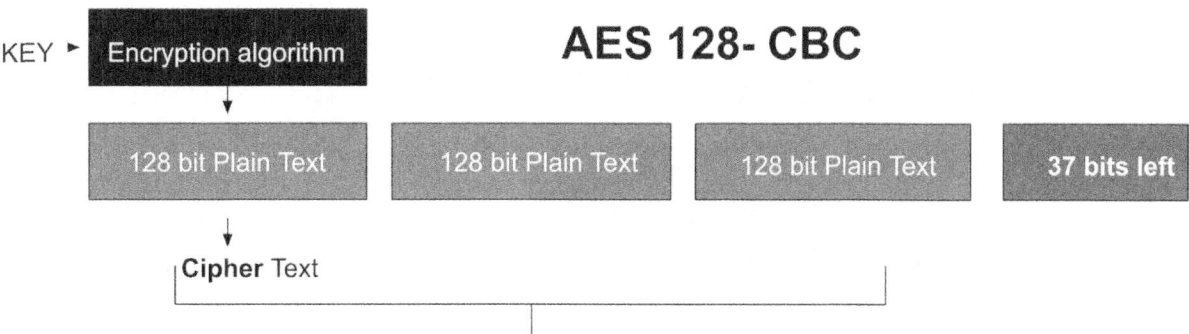

We fill the remainder, with Padding", Which is nothing more than predefined value as all 1, or all 0

ECB is one of the most Un secure methods to aggregate blocks, as we can see a repetition very Fast, the same plain text is being encrypted with the same key, so nowadays, we use other modes of operation that makes it much more secure, as **CBC (cipher block chaining)**

In **CBC**, we use another factor, an **IV** (Initialization Vector, a pseudo-random value). The IV has to be sent to the other side, as it is part of the encryption process

- We start and XOR the plain text with the IV
- And then we encrypt it with the secret KEY

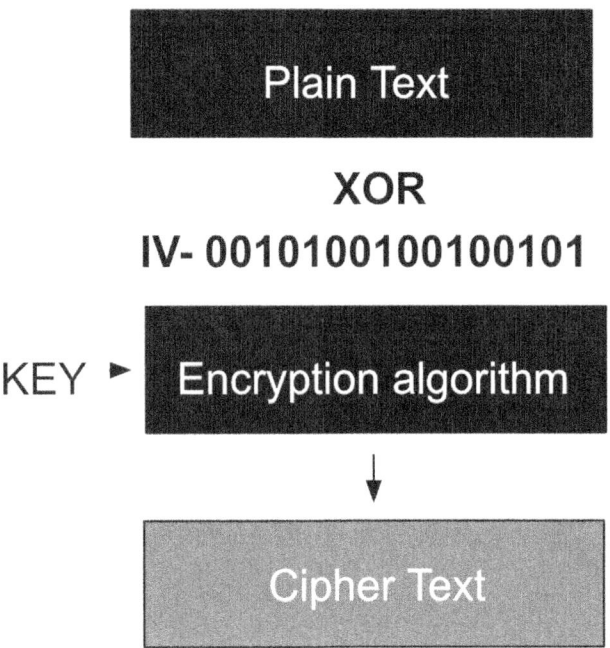

And then our **block 1 ciphertext** is being XORed with the plain text of **block 2** and then encrypted and so on

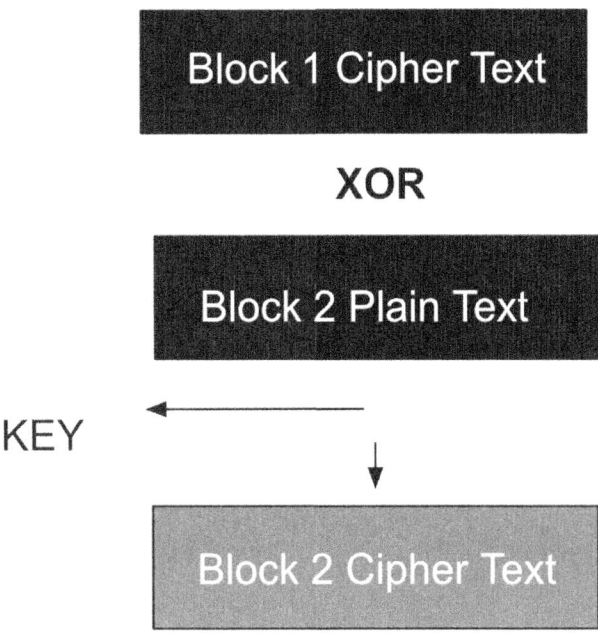

Due to the chaining of the ciphered blocks, from one block to the other, the block always changes, making it much more secure

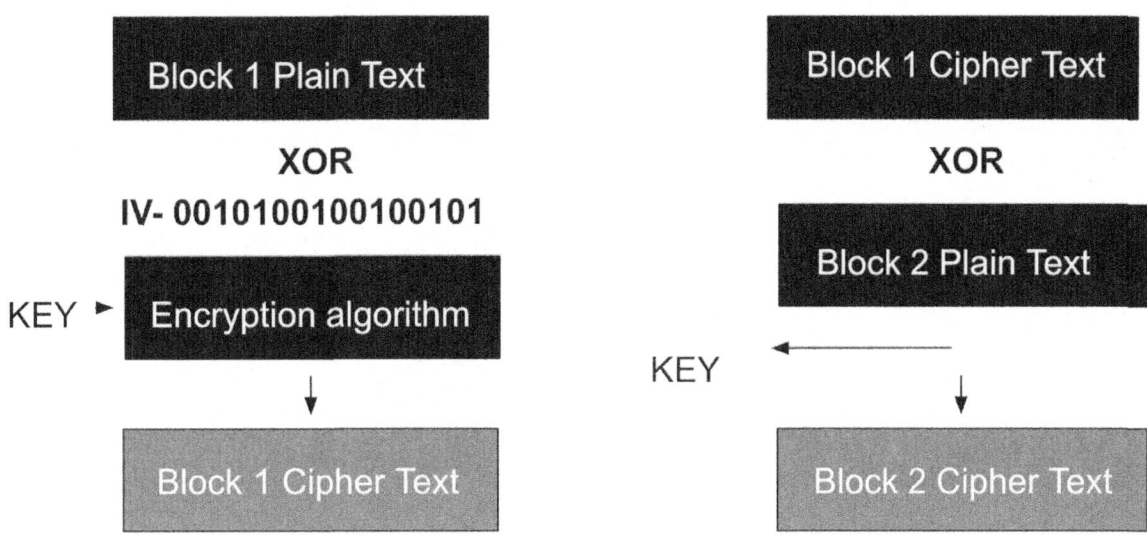

Modern Cipher - Algorithm operation

Modern Algorithm are using different operations, time after time when they encrypt data

What kind of operations:

- Throwing away some bits
- Rearranging the bits (using substitution and transitioning)
- Splitting the key data into 2 parts
- Swapping between the parts
- Shifting the bits left and write

01010010010100000011111001000

01010010010100   Splitting   000011111001000

000011111001000   Swapping   01010010010100

000101111001000   Shifting   01010010010100

Data is being permutated time after time...in Cryptography we call that "Rounds" in DES cipher we use 16 rounds

Let's Look at one step, which is the permutation of the Bitstream

Original 4bit key
16 possible keys   **1010101110011 10**

Permutation Table   **12,5,1,7,4,6,2,9,11,10,13,3,14,8,1**

Our original bitstream is being rearranged, according to a new mapping, where bit number 1, is repositioned at the 12 places, bit number 2 at the 5th place, and so on

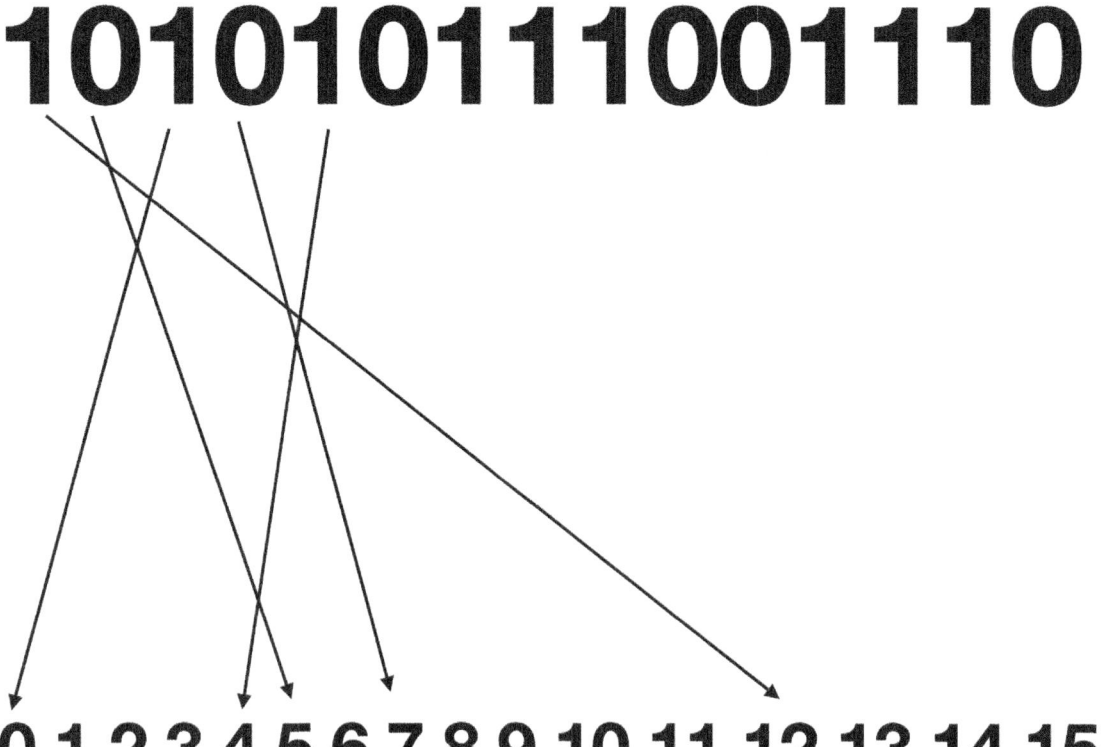

Asymmetric Encryption

Asymmetric ciphers, or encryption, are used everywhere nowadays, and they suggest a new idea. If up until now we have had symmetry between the 2 keys. Asymmetric suggest 2 different keys, one that will be **Public**, and the other one **Private**

Asymmetric encryption solved the key distribution issue. , sending the secret key to the other side which possesses security risk
We also use Asymmetric encryption as a mean for integrity and authentication, which are 2 topics, that I will go through in my second book

Let's look at it through an example

Eve wants to send a message to Bob

She writes down the message, she encrypts it using its own symmetric key
And then, when it is encrypted, she sent it to Bob.

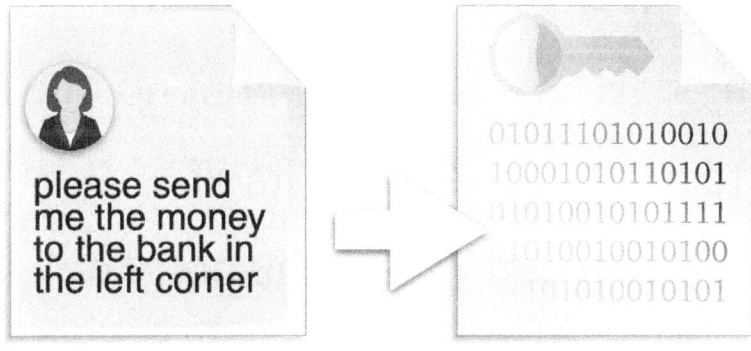

Now, Bob knows the secret symmetric key that she uses.
And he decrypts the message.

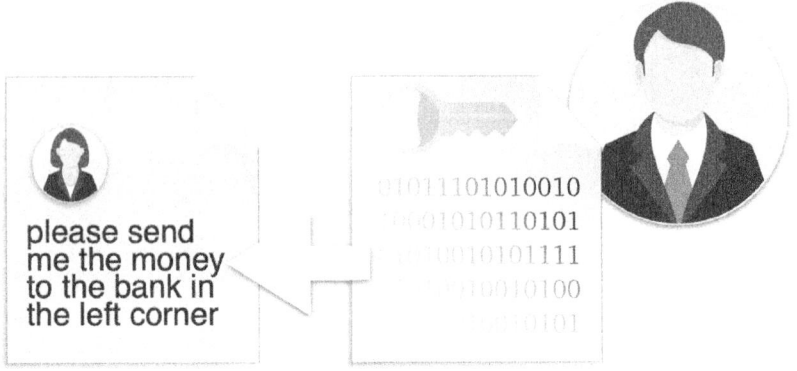

If you think about it, we actually achieved only one thing we encrypted, the message. But then again, we have other challenges.

The first challenge, how can we deliver the key between Eve and Bob, Let's assume that even Bob doesn't live close by.

The second challenge is how can we tell that the message wasn't modified. How can we tell that no one actually modified the text of the message itself?

And the **third challenge**. How can we tell the person who pretends to be Eve is really Eve?

To address those challenges, we use Asymmetric encryption,

When Eve encrypted her message she actually used a symmetric encryption key that was known also to Bob.

Bob also knows, which cipher algorithm is used to encrypt the message.

> You can generate random 128bit key using a free tool openssl with the rand command
>
> ```
> ofers-MBP:~ ofer$ openssl rand -hex 32
> bbcb7ea478254e25aad45acdf726bdde295bfd899f9fe3327dd535b1646050ae
> ofers-MBP:~ ofer$
> ```
>
> **Each Hexdecimal digit has a 4bit value , so 32 hexdecimal number is actually a 128bit key**

On Asymmetric encryption, Eve is generating key pairs. They may look similar, but they are actually different, (mathematically related)

The first Key is the **Private Key**, it is actually the secret key that Eve needs to keep in a secret place.

                                                  Private   **Public**

The second Key is the **Public Key**, and as the name suggests, it is public, everyone can use that key.

Eve sends the Public Key to Bob

When Bob gets the key, he can use it for asymmetric encryption of his own messages

And as expected, decrypt any messages that were encrypted using the public key.

Generate Public and Private Key

If we go back to **open SSL**, let's just write down **"openssl genrsa 2048"** RSA, one of the algorithms of asymmetric encryption. And we'll use the **2048 bit key**.

```
[ofers-MBP:~ ofer$ openssl genrsa 2048
Generating RSA private key, 2048 bit long modulus
.............+++
.............................+++
e is 65537 (0x10001)
-----BEGIN RSA PRIVATE KEY-----
MIIEowIBAAKCAQEAq1RLEshkfdTpe4mAjzCwhi6Wyle93sGcrtJmzQ1ZeLsH0adz
TjMi+vADGNsRRDWpICiu4mClHmRjpM3HeiONF4MVw0BKFPAdrEea0z1kcUOKgDNg
Yg3HKxVdiiicCdautBLYedmrkf0fdLItoPV5IqdVMRSZ+FkiLz80892ByJbE/si+
LVc27UmayKyf4yUvtX3Ly1iccpoZLqs2wsYjRv11EykwR4D7hvMfyAbfdzifK3VP
bUZxAgU3mgjNuObfQC4U9BTKBuQnlJJhb19eOmVCkUz88fcG61z4XVdsbsZ/QK+k
GvcwshaYEZs/FO7+STRj7KAZ4ZysPL6ZsrCWLwIDAQABAoIBAQCqv7iOQJ8+dQo4
76HrkyfqotXvVSDKt4TTCqgfpjVMSIITZWJaRkaPdtJvXCzKIPysKz+YJ5+IOZ7B
KcCrLnE4RJFU5WavlVrNTxOzgVTwONL4z7s4HekoPAPcZHqWp5m3p6yNS+1c8rr9
z3IAH4UZj1EtOA33X8Xc9o5smI72/AF0DKaE6l96agKNO77TP+23GW0xytJBoNJh
JGv+hUYweftC37ni9rkFS22MoJto1eJLF+rSIk1m2y+d+CSaw7bPXFU3k03l3vd1
Pve9XdiRKKXWsbGwRFiEfK0rW174kqg1d7vgizOFkThPh3IjpcSTa9yJwbHhbady
3JBFzXmhAoGBAOAYD0l1JJ0ZL21v//y6J4JvaLB+r7gwoSjF4Al/HEgKV7lsIh3w
HSG2vnUdO/wrhUs/e7F2hJtxmHufNa8b9aMrf4X5XuudD7kwJtrqWysOSifOlqH8
RCK364MxM/TOjptrctO2fIZkNe2RAMFGaTRIe0NjhiWyLIYRe5GRL1URAoGBAMO5
BucCS60U76is5gyqE1wG6m8q166aNAdpsCXLRagGr/rCpu6V1SWipOKzG+k0W+JN
6fSHb5wLnH277xEqbQ5mK8N9IfA8CglW+H05qI8ge9tJkz9E1SwCmhmaDdCbFtWD
wIbAoSNzsZH3rIa1HPJFS+NFmHG+tUv8ZI7whDc/AoGAMvjmCURvBpji89ak+Jxz
PjUPMA4w9AmDrt2Lfz19dll76L5S6FJknfWOTt9OdKaFlD8laJFXym/FSmFFecY3
Ul0jjZrSX2+DUxFD1Um3YQzIC1PvaXsTGH6TQG0hr06Im4uOO9/nZT5IEfiInm3g
ojbWatapfcuQWxKA8/R9OrECgYBlMJUj/CjZ/HgHshRiOdA2hRDRlsnZ6Lm7l2XN
tHF39LUpJVgfA/ImOhebaVSl1j8nGnc5yIfomow26WIpctDdX++Ca4CPbssVlxRz
0cqW7Ql8D2cEj/bSgSng0KgR0Q0WKL7yLEdjR95nhDB7mMm1bCRXBVVSgXHELmJj
EHCbCwKBgEdozFNoiz9c4vgUIRf2EtOTpztG7ieWfEVpKH2zhCXQfMfRBGq7ZVlV
PkIZ8oa6x/CY6YzYmIR+eO/IlA4sksFjGETdgGj1+y2AfrJsOTLe46D00NafPKZx
04/Du1KdX4nolwqIiKm7Ey/LYefbpHqW9NWxOUcQuS4C+iNg7NQQ
-----END RSA PRIVATE KEY-----
ofers-MBP:~ ofer$
```

That's our **Private key**

We can actually generate the public key from the private key that we just generated.

```
ofers-MBP:~ ofer$ cat rsa.public
-----BEGIN PUBLIC KEY-----
MIIBIjANBgkqhkiG9w0BAQEFAAOCAQ8AMIIBCgKCAQEAojJLp7FbBR1o0BH2CX53
YL6YjbASiHKCFgC18xqsRkvktog3tx4QjdiJ05UjUbmqtRyq5swicKxlhhbN+j2s
6Ujxx3owKPRqf7ySoLgDE22YBAbmm54Zf0grp/TA89k/0FBoU00WSIRkdGjyN+y5
R4VyV46ND9jvjTB2mWm37QucTOOIriRyj6H5h4pO976q0dovxYsc69aXZfFaUKy7
CZ4tHK2PBsb5WtPqe3umEPwkDRX2eS8Qz1O3x/iM6V6g3sG0WWQMpBCWhOOWl+X6
c59RH0XLNFXCgKvH/oY0/LMpF1HRLu7ZMngh5ofRTjSpr2JmWU2F82UtGMYvvUqp
CwIDAQAB
-----END PUBLIC KEY-----
ofers-MBP:~ ofer$
```

That's our **Public key**

Remember The public key is sent to Bob

Bob gets his public key and decrypts messages. Now, think about it, the fact that only this public key can decrypt messages from Eve, suggests that the message actually came from Eve.

That's one way to authenticate the other side.

Although asymmetric encryption has been created, it is not used to encrypt the session itself. The Date that is being sent from Eve to Bob, and vice versa, is being encrypted using symmetric keys

Why?

One of the reasons is the size of the keys and thus the speed of encrypting and decrypting large amounts of data

The private and the public keys are used for many reasons in modern communication, one of them, which is related to our topic, is to encrypt the session (their 2way communication) keys, the symmetric encryption keys that will encrypt the data.

Once the two parties, (Eve and Bob) want to encrypt their session, they negotiate, which symmetric encryption will they use AES128, 3DES…

> Once the two parties, (Eve and Bob) want to encrypt their session, they negotiate, which symmetric encryption will they use AES128, 3DES…

When the decision is made

Eve generates a symmetric key a pseudo-random key.

Eve encrypts it using the Asymmetric key (her private key)

Bob get the encrypted message. Open it, with his own public key, and now he knows what is the symmetric key that Eve will use to encrypt the Data

Final Words

You have just Finished "The secrets book - cryptography for beginners"

I hope that you enjoyed the journey. My aim was to give you a head start on

Cryptography essentials

Sincerely yours

Ofer Shmueli

Printed in Great Britain
by Amazon